Sequestered

Charles Elliott Newbold, Jr.

All scriptures are taken from the New King James Version. Copyright © 1982 by Thomas Nelson, Inc. Used by permission. All rights reserved.

Cover design by Mary DeChellis

For additional reading by Charles Elliott Newbold, Jr. see: www.charlesnewbold.com

Copyright © 2016 Charles Elliott Newbold, Jr.

All rights reserved.

ISBN: 9780997706000

TABLE OF CONTENTS

Preface	i
Introduction	1
The Trial	4
God's Finished Works	12
I, I AM	19
Witnesses of Jesus	30
Believe	39
The Son of God	49
Eternal Life	66
In Him	74
The Holy Spirit	81
Love	86
Summation and Sequestration	97

TABLE OF CONTENTS

Preface	i
Introduction	1
The Trial	4
God's Finished Works	12
I, I AM	19
Witnesses of Jesus	30
Believe	39
The Son of God	49
Eternal Life	66
In Him	74
The Holy Spirit	81
Love	86
Summation and Sequestration	97

Preface

The themes written in this book had been gestating in me for years. I had prayed for the day I would be able to give them birth in written form. I consider it a great honor and privilege to share these with you in writing.

The bulk of the narrative comes from scripture which has been paraphrased in the interest of drawing out these various themes which I have identified as Witnesses. Nevertheless, this study is no substitute for reading the gospel of John as written.

Moreover, I have purposely stayed within the text of John's gospel to relate the points the apostle wanted to make in his account of Jesus' life. I have not referenced any other scripture beyond the content of this gospel.

I have attempted to give an account of what John has said and his quotes of Jesus and have minimized my own interpretations.

The manner in which I present this study is normally called "poetic license." Call it what you will. I have taken the liberty to stage this study in a courtroom setting with the author of the gospel of John serving as the Defense Attorney for Jesus.

Use this as a study guide individually or in a group.

Introduction

The trial of the ages occurred in Jerusalem over two thousand years ago. Yet, at the time of its occurrence, most of the world did not know about it. It must have seemed quite insignificant on the global scene.

John, the beloved apostle of Jesus, wrote this testimony in what is called the Gospel of John. Perhaps you have read it several times. His narrative is ingenious and fascinating to say the least. The Holy Spirit, through the apostle John, laid down layer upon layer of revealed knowledge, often requiring divine inspiration to see them.

The accused was a man called Jesus [Yeshua in Hebrew]. His accusers [also viewed as His Prosecutors] were the religious and political leaders of His day, commonly referred to in scriptures as "the Jews."

This Jesus was accused of blasphemy because He claimed to be the Son of God, and worse yet, to be God.

John, in this portrayal of Jesus' trial, is the defense lawyer. His task is to bring forth witnesses on behalf of the accused to prove His innocence of blasphemy by presenting evidence that He was who He claimed to be—the Messiah, the Son of God, even God.

John's account of this trial and his defense was written down years later after Jesus' actual trial, judgment, and crucifixion. John was not trying to change the outcome. Jesus had to be crucified in such a manner in order to fulfill scripture and the ultimate, eternal intentions of God, the Father.

Rather, his defense is targeted to all peoples of all times who look back upon this man and who will, in one way or the other, hand down their own verdict as they answer these questions: "Who is this man who claimed to be the Messiah, the Son of God, and even God?" "What am I going to believe about Him? Moreover, what am I going to do about Him?"

In the process of reviewing this case in these studies, we will revisit many of the same accounts, emphasizing different aspects within them. Several of these threads of evidence or claims are introduced in the opening words of John's gospel; namely, *I, I AM*, Abiding in Him, Life and Light, Witness, Faith, and the New Birth. These threads (called as witnesses) form the chapters in this study.

John makes bold introductory claims about Jesus in the beginning, then returns to the foundation of his case and builds toward an ultimate, concluding argument.

Who is John?

John was the son of Zebedee, the brother of James, both of whom were called early on by Jesus to be apostles. Matthew 10:2. He was the one who leaned back on Jesus' breast at the last supper. John 13:25. He is the one who wrote the gospel of John, the three letters, and the book of Revelation. He is the one of whom Jesus said to Peter, "If I will that he remain till I come, what is that to you? You follow Me." He is the one to whom Jesus turned to care for His mother. John 19:26-27.

In John's own words he acknowledged himself as "the disciple who testifies of these things, and wrote these things; and we know that his testimony is true." John 21:22-24.

It has been left to legend to say how, where, and when John died.

John has been called apostle, evangelist, and theologian. For the purposes of this study, we shall think of him as the Defense Attorney.

The Setting

The Trial

Dusk settled over the garden where Jesus and His disciples had retreated. Judas, in the act of betraying Jesus, led the detachment of officers from the chief priests and Pharisees to Him in the garden. They approached with lanterns, torches, and weapons to arrest Him.

Jesus, knowing all the things that were to happen, faced off with them asking, "Whom are you seeking?"

They answered, "Jesus of Nazareth."

Jesus said, "*I, I AM.*"[1]

Judas, who betrayed Him, also stood with the detachment.

When Jesus said to them, "*I, I AM,*" they drew back and fell to the ground.

He asked them again, "Whom are you seeking?"

Again they answered, "Jesus of Nazareth."

"I have told you that *I, I AM*. Therefore, if you seek Me,

---

[1] The "*I, I AM*" witness will be called to the witness stand later on in the trial.

case and builds toward an ultimate, concluding argument.

Who is John?

John was the son of Zebedee, the brother of James, both of whom were called early on by Jesus to be apostles. Matthew 10:2. He was the one who leaned back on Jesus' breast at the last supper. John 13:25. He is the one who wrote the gospel of John, the three letters, and the book of Revelation. He is the one of whom Jesus said to Peter, "If I will that he remain till I come, what is that to you? You follow Me." He is the one to whom Jesus turned to care for His mother. John 19:26-27.

In John's own words he acknowledged himself as "the disciple who testifies of these things, and wrote these things; and we know that his testimony is true." John 21:22-24.

It has been left to legend to say how, where, and when John died.

John has been called apostle, evangelist, and theologian. For the purposes of this study, we shall think of him as the Defense Attorney.

The Setting

The Trial

Dusk settled over the garden where Jesus and His disciples had retreated. Judas, in the act of betraying Jesus, led the detachment of officers from the chief priests and Pharisees to Him in the garden. They approached with lanterns, torches, and weapons to arrest Him.

Jesus, knowing all the things that were to happen, faced off with them asking, "Whom are you seeking?"

They answered, "Jesus of Nazareth."

Jesus said, "*I, I AM.*"[1]

Judas, who betrayed Him, also stood with the detachment.

When Jesus said to them, "*I, I AM,*" they drew back and fell to the ground.

He asked them again, "Whom are you seeking?"

Again they answered, "Jesus of Nazareth."

"I have told you that *I, I AM*. Therefore, if you seek Me,

---

[1] The "*I, I AM*" witness will be called to the witness stand later on in the trial.

let these go their way," that the saying might be fulfilled which He spoke, "Of those whom You gave Me I have lost none."

Peter impulsively drew his sword and cut off the right ear of Malchus, the servant of the high priest.

Jesus halted Peter saying, "Put your sword into the sheath. Shall I not drink the cup which My Father has given Me?"

This incident marked the official beginning of the most famed trial of all times. Yet, comparatively speaking, only a trifling number of people huddled around the cross on that day even knew of it.

Annas   John 18: 12-14

This military detachment along with the captain and the officers of the Jews arrested Jesus and bound Him. They led Him to Annas who was the father-in-law of Caiaphas, the high priest that year.

Caiaphas was he who, speaking by the Holy Spirit, had previously advised the Jews it was expedient that one man should die for the people. John 11:47-52.

Caiaphas John 18:24

Annas sent Jesus bound to the high priest, Caiaphas, accusing Jesus of calling Himself, the King of the Jews.

Pilate   John 18:28-40

By early morning, Jesus had been led from Caiaphas to

the Praetorium[2] to go before Pilate. The Jews did not go into the Praetorium for fear they would be defiled before eating the Passover.

Pilate went out to the Jews and asked, "What accusation do you bring against this Man?"

They answered, "If He were not an evildoer, we would not have delivered Him up to you."

Pilate responded, "You take Him and judge Him according to your law."

They answered, "It is not lawful for us to put anyone to death."

Uncertain by all of this, Pilate went back into the Praetorium to further interrogate Jesus, "Are you the King of the Jews?"

Jesus pricking Pilate's conscience asked in return, "Are you speaking for yourself about this, or did others tell you this concerning Me?"

Pilate fired back, "Am I a Jew? Your own nation and the chief priests have delivered You to me. What have You done?"

Jesus made clear to Pilate that His kingdom was not of this world. If His kingdom were of this world, His servants would have fought back and He would not have been delivered to the Jews.

---

[2] The Praetorium is the headquarters in a Roman camp, the tent of the commander-in-chief. It has also been translated "hall of judgment."

"Are you a king then?"

"You say that I am a king. For this cause I was born, and for this cause I have come into the world, that I should bear witness to the truth. Everyone who is of the truth hears My voice."

"What is truth?" Pilate shrugs it off and goes back out to the Jews, exonerating Jesus. "I find no fault in Him at all."

The crowd and Barabbas   John 18:39-40

Pilate handed the decision back into the hands of the crowd. "You have a custom that I should release someone to you at the Passover. Do you therefore want me to release to you the King of the Jews?"

The crowd all cried out again, saying, "Not this Man, but Barabbas!" Now Barabbas was a robber.

Pilate and the crowd John 19:1-16

Why Pilate scourged Jesus since he had found no fault in Him is hard to reason. Yet, that scriptures might be fulfilled, He stood in Pilate's court, suffering the pain and humiliation of His scoffers. The soldiers thrust a twisted crown of thorns upon His head, draped Him with a purple robe and jeered, "Hail, King of the Jews!" They struck Him with their hands.

Pilate took Jesus out to the crowd and reaffirmed his opinion. "Behold, I am bringing Him out to you, that you may know that I find no fault in Him."

Jesus stumbled out bleeding from the crown of thorns and donned with the purple robe. Pilate swept his hand forward, presenting Him to the crowd announcing, "Behold the Man!"

The chief priest and officers declared their final verdict. When they saw Him, they cried out, "Crucify, crucify!"

Still, Pilate pronounced his final verdict on the man, insisting they take Him and crucify Him. "I find no fault in Him."

Pilate grew more fearful of the situation when the Jews responded to him, "We have a law, and according to our law He ought to die, because He made Himself the Son of God."

Therefore, when Pilate was all the more afraid when he heard that saying. He returned to the Praetorian, and asked Jesus, "Where are You from?"

Jesus did not answer.

"Are You not speaking to me? Do You not know that I have power to crucify You, and power to release You?"

"You could have no power at all against Me unless it had been given you from above. Therefore the one who delivered Me to you has the greater sin."

Despite every effort by Pilate to release Jesus, he ultimately buckled under the threat of Jews who threatened, "If you let this Man go, you are not

Caesar's friend. Whoever makes himself a king speaks against Caesar."

Pilate brought Jesus out and sat down in the judgment seat in a place that is called Pavement, but in Hebrew, Gabbatha. It was the Preparation Day of the Passover, about the sixth hour. Pilate said to the Jews, "Behold your King!"

Rejecting Jesus as their King, the Jews called out, "Away with Him, away with Him! Crucify Him!"

Pilate put the crowd in the jury box, demanding their verdict. "Shall I crucify your King?"

The chief priests pronounced the verdict for the crowd. "We have no king but Caesar!" What an astounding declaration to make!

Pilate delivered Jesus to them to be crucified. They took Jesus and led Him away.

Golgotha John 19:17-42

The verdict of the Jews, the evasiveness of Pilate, and the maddening crowd sent the King of the Jews to His death on a Roman cross.

Jesus stumbled out, carrying His own cross to a place called Skull, Golgotha in Hebrew. They crucified Him with two others, one to His left and the other to His right.

Following the hoisting of the cross, the soldiers each tore Jesus' garment and divided it among themselves except for the tunic. It was woven from top to bottom in one piece and too valuable to be torn. Instead, they cast lots for it. This fulfilled the scripture prophecy, "They divided My garments among them, and for My clothing they cast lots."

Jesus mother, His mother's sister, Mary the wife of Clopas, and Mary Magdalene were standing by the cross. When Jesus saw His mother and John (the disciple whom He loved) standing by, He said to her, "Woman, behold your son!" Then He said to John, "Behold your mother! And from that hour that disciple took her to his own home." John would have learned much from her about the early life of Jesus.

The final moments on the cross may have seemed ordinary, but everything and every word spoken fulfilled scripture, even when voicing His anguish saying, "I thirst!" They filled a sponge with sour wine and hyssop, and put it on his mouth. When Jesus received it, He cried out, "It is finished." He bowed His head and gave up His spirit.

Because His crucifixion occurred on the Preparation Day, a high day before Passover, the bodies could not remain on the cross. Rather than breaking Jesus' leg to make sure He was dead, one of the soldiers pierced His side with a spear causing blood and water to flow out.

John witnessed it all. He wrote, "He who has seen has testified, and his testimony is true; and he knows that he is telling the truth, so that you may believe. These things were done that the Scripture should be fulfilled. "Not one of His bones shall be broken." Psalm 34:20. And again, "They shall look on Him whom they pierced." Zechariah 12:10.

Following His death on the cross, Joseph of Arimathea, a disciple of Jesus, obtained permission from Pilate to take His body. Nicodemus was there. They anointed it with myrrh and aloes, wrapped Him in strips of linen with spices, and placed it in a nearby new tomb.

Ironically, thinking they were charging Jesus with a crime, they inadvertently charged Him with the truth. He was guilty in part of the charge. They charged Him of blasphemy for saying that He was the Son of God. The part about Him being the Son of God was true. The part about Him blaspheming was false because He was the Son of God. His sentence echoes today. "Crucify Him, Crucify Him." Any other verdict would have run contrary to the eternal will and purposes of God, the Father.

That was then, but not the end. Every one of us, Jew and Gentile, male and female of every nation, tribe, and generation from that day to this find ourselves sequestered in the jury room of our own hearts, faced with the piercing question, "Do I believe?"

Witness One:
God's Finished Works

I portray John as the defense attorney for Jesus. Liberty is taken to stage the Gospel of John in the setting of a trial. Various witnesses are called to testify on behalf of the accused.

The historical trial is over. The verdict is in. The sentence has been carried out. Yet, in keeping with the irony of this whole event, the trial continues.

The irony is this: The Accusers said Jesus was guilty of blasphemy because He *said* He was the Son of God. John, the Defender of Jesus, agreed in part. Jesus was guilty in saying He *is* the Son of God, but He is not guilty of blasphemy because He really is the Son of God.

John called his first witness to the stand. The identity of this first witness is *God's Finished Works*.

The Setting   Chapters 5-6

Jesus went up to Jerusalem to the pool of Bethesda during a feast of the Jews. The blind, lame, and paralyzed lay waiting for an angel to come down to stir up the water. Whoever stepped in first was healed.

Jesus singled out a man who had suffered an infirmity

for thirty-eight years and asked if he wanted to be made well. Of course, he did. Jesus told him to pick up his bed and walk. Immediately the man was made well. He picked up his bed and walked.

No mention is made of Jesus healing any of the others at the pool. What's the big deal? Ah! It was the Sabbath. It was unlawful for anyone to carry certain items, especially one's bed. Did Jesus overlook this technicality? Hardly! He did it deliberately. Sure, he had compassion for the sick man, but He also had another motive in mind. He intentionally provoked a debate with the Jews. John devoted considerable space relating this event.

Later, Jesus found the man in the Temple and said to him, "See, you have been made well. Sin no more, lest a worse thing come upon you." The man then told the Jews it was Jesus who had healed him. The Jews persecuted Jesus and sought to kill Him because He had done these things on the Sabbath.

John presents a seven-point defense that should persuade any juror inclined to believe. Notice the progression of thought.

*Point One: Jesus and the Father are working together
John 5:17*

Jesus answered them, "My Father has been working until now, and I have been working."

With this outrageous assertion, the Jews sought to kill

Him all the more, not only because He broke the Sabbath, but He also said God was His Father, making Himself equal with God. If God is His Father, that makes Him a son of God.

Jesus had already told His disciples while at Jacob's well in Samaria, "My food is to do the will of Him who sent Me, and to finish His work." John 4:34.

Later on, Jesus punctuated His point by healing a man who had been blind from birth. His disciples asked Him if this man's blindness was due to his sin or that of his parents. Jesus said, "Neither." He added, "I must work the works of Him who sent Me while it is day; the night is coming when no one can work." John 9:1-4.

Point Two: Jesus does only what He sees the Father doing   John 5:19-23

Moreover, Jesus said to them, "Most assuredly, I say to you, the Son can do nothing of Himself, but what He sees the Father do; for whatever He does, the Son also does in like manner." He explained: "For the Father loves the Son, and shows Him all things that He Himself does; and He will show Him greater works than these, that you may marvel. For as the Father raises the dead and gives life to them, even so the Son gives life to whom He will."

The "Father judges no one, but has committed all judgment to the Son, that all should honor the Son just as they honor the Father. He who does not honor the

Son does not honor the Father who sent Him."

Point Three: Jesus is the work of God   John 5:24-26

Everything the Father wanted to do for the salvation of the world was accomplished in Jesus. Jesus explained, "Most assuredly, I say to you, he who hears My word and believes in Him who sent Me has everlasting life, and shall not come into judgment, but has passed from death into life. Most assuredly, I say to you, the hour is coming, and now is, when the dead will hear the voice of the Son of God; and those who hear will live. For as the Father has life in Himself, so He has granted the Son to have life in Himself."

The apostle, John, declared this from the beginning of his defense. "In the beginning was the Word, and the Word was with God, and the Word was God. He was in the beginning with God. All things were made through Him, and without Him nothing was made that was made. In Him was life, and the life was the light of men." John 1:1-4.

Then, Jesus re-asserted, "I can of Myself do nothing. As I hear, I judge; and My judgment is righteous, because I do not seek My own will but the will of the Father who sent Me." John 5:30.

Point Four: Jesus finished the works of God   John 5:36

Jesus pointed to John the Baptist as a viable witness, but declared that the greatest witness to His being the Son of God was based on the works that He Himself did. "But I have a greater witness than John's; for the works which the Father has given Me to finish—the very works that I do—bear witness of Me, that the Father has sent Me."

The proof that the works Jesus had been given belong to Him to finish was punctuated by two major miracles. He fed five thousand men by multiplying five loaves of barley and two fish belonging to a young lad. To top that, He walked on water. John 6:1-21.

> *Point Five: Jesus is the finished work of God   John 6:31-35*

Jesus not only gave them bread miraculously, but also explained that He was the bread that came down from heaven.

They said, "Our fathers ate the manna in the desert; as it is written, 'He gave them bread from heaven to eat.'"

Jesus explained, "Most assuredly, I say to you, Moses did not give you the bread from heaven, but My Father gives you the true bread from heaven. For the bread of God is He who comes down from heaven and gives life to the world."

Then they begged Him, "Lord, give us this bread always."

"I am the bread of life. He who comes to Me shall never hunger, and he who believes in Me shall never thirst."

By declaring, "I am the bread of life," Jesus illustrated how He is the finished work of God.

The final words of Jesus on the cross in His earthly life confirm this. He said, "It is finished." He was not referring to His earthly, physical life. He was not saying, "Well, it is all over now." This declaration was in the context of the previous statement by John saying, "After this, Jesus, knowing that all things were now accomplished, that the Scripture might be fulfilled, said, 'I thirst!'"

He knew He had accomplished all things that the Father had sent Him to accomplish. He bowed His head and gave up His spirit. John 19:28-30.

Point Six: Our part in the work of God   John 6:28-29

Those who were seeking Jesus asked, "What shall we do, that we may work the works of God?" Jesus answered them, "This is the work of God, that you believe in Him whom He sent."

No other stipulation was required of them. Remember John's reason for writing? "That we may believe Jesus is the Christ, the Son of God, and that believing we may have life in His name." John 20:31.

Point Seven: We become the finished work of God. John 6:47

We are the work the Father intends to complete in Jesus. "Most assuredly, I say to you, he who believes in

Me has everlasting life."

Point eight: Greater works   John 14:12-14

We who believe become the vessels through which Jesus does even greater works.

Jesus was comforting His disciples, telling them that He would be going away to prepare a place for them with the promise that He will return again and receive them unto Himself. He assured them that from then on they would know the Father because they had seen Him.

Then, Jesus made an astounding promise. "He who believes in Me, the works that I do he will do also; and greater works than these he will do, because I go to My Father. And whatever you ask in My name, that I will do, that the Father may be glorified in the Son. If you ask anything in My name, I will do it."

Greater works than what He has done! We might think we are the ones doing the greater works, but given the context of this witness, it is Jesus who does the greater works through us.

The "God's Finished Works" witness steps down from the witness stand, but remains under oath and can be recalled anytime.

Witness Two

I, I AM

John calls the *I, I AM* witness to the stand.

The question before us here is simple. Who, then, exactly is this Jesus in whom John invites us to believe?

Members of the body of Christ fall out with each other over that *in which* we believe. It is difficult to fall out with each other over *in whom* we believe. Certainly, what we believe about Jesus is important; nevertheless, we are not saved by *in what* we believe, rather by *in whom* we believe.

John's defense in this courtroom boldly testified regarding the person of Jesus, and it is not about getting our doctrines right. John wants us to know in no uncertain terms exactly who this Jesus is. He stated it in his opening statement. John 1:1-4.

Read this slowly and deliberately, realizing that John was talking about Jesus.

"In the beginning was the Word [Jesus],

"And the Word was with God,

"And the Word was God.

"He was in the beginning with God.

"All things were made through Him,

"And without Him nothing was made that was made.

"In Him was life,

"And the life was the light of men." John 1:1-4.

John had no problem believing Jesus was both God and the Son of God. Neither should we. It may not be logical; nevertheless, we take it at face value.

How, then, can one read this opening statement, believing in the divine inspiration of God's word, and not say Jesus was God? John made this bold declaration, and then visibly addressed this theme throughout. It is the "*I, I AM*" theme. In every case, Jesus made this claim of Himself.

I, I AM

First, we explore the implication of the *I, I AM* terminology. The English letters for these Greek words are *ego eimi*. *Ego eimi* occurs 23 times in John's gospel. In every case, Jesus used this identification to explain His saving relationship with His believers. These are covered in order of their occurrence in John.

Ego eimi is accurately translated, *I, I AM*. *Ego* means, "I." *Eimi* means, "I am." They are used together for emphasis. The use of this emphasis by John is deliberate.

Most translations simply render this, "I am." Such is the case in the metaphors below. This fails to communicate the deeper message intended here, that Jesus is God—Yahweh.

The name Yahweh was given to Moses while tending the flock of his father-in-law Jethro, the priest of Midian. Moses came upon the burning bush. The angel of the Lord appeared to Moses and God said, "I am the God of your father—the God of Abraham, the God of Isaac, and the God of Jacob." At this time and place, God commissioned Moses to set His people free from Egyptian bondage.

Moses asked, "When I come to the children of Israel and say to them, 'The God of your fathers has sent me to you,' and they say to me, 'What is His name?' What shall I say to them?"

"God answered Moses, 'I AM WHO I AM.' Thus you shall say to the children of Israel, 'I AM' has sent me to you."

The English for this Hebrew tetragram is YHWH. Some scholars believe this means, "The Being." Others have said it means, "I Am that I Am." Throughout the Old Testament YHWH has been translated LORD with small caps. Wherever we come across LORD, we can know that it is in reference to YHWH. This is the name of God as revealed to Moses.

The Greek translators of the Septuagint expressly used the *ego eimi* (*I, I AM*) to identify God's name in this passage. The Septuagint is a Greek translation of the Hebrew Bible. It was made for Greek-speaking Jews who lived in Egypt in the 3rd and 2nd centuries before Christ. Early Christian assemblies adopted it for use. This is the very name Jesus used, claiming to be this God who revealed Himself to Moses.

As we read below, we could rightfully substitute Yahweh in each instance where Jesus said, *I, I AM*.

The first occurrence of the I, I AM witness is John 4:26

Jesus had been talking to the Samaritan woman at the well. She said, "I know that Messiah is coming who is called Christ. When He comes, He will tell us all things." Jesus said to her, "I who speak to you am *He*." The translator added *He*. It is not in the original. Correctly translated it would read, "I who speak to you *I, I AM*." Christ is Yahweh.

The second occurrence of the I, I AM witness is in John 6:48-59

Jesus declared, "*I, I AM* the bread of life."

Jesus reminded them in this illustration that their fathers in the wilderness ate the manna and died. He, on the other hand, is the living bread that comes down from heaven and whoever eats of this bread, Jesus, will live forever.

The third occurrence of the I, I AM witness is in John 8:12

Jesus declared, "*I, I AM* the light of the world." Whoever

follows Him will not walk in darkness, but have the light of life.

The fourth occurrence of the I, I AM witness is in John 8:13-20

The Pharisees accused Him saying, "You bear witness of yourself. Your witness is not true."

Jesus answered, "*I, I AM* who bears witness of Myself, and the Father who sent Me bears witness of Me."

"Where is Your Father?"

"You know neither Me nor My Father. If you had known Me, you would have known My Father also."

The fifth occurrence of the I, I AM witness is in John 8:21-24

The Jews were still testing Jesus. He told them He was going away and where He was going they could not go. They thought He was going to kill Himself.

He answered, "You are from beneath; *I, I AM* from above. You are of this world; *I, I AM* not of this world. Therefore I said to you that you will die in your sins; for if you do not believe that *I, I AM*, you will die in your sins." Interpreted: If you do not believe that Jesus is Yahweh, you will die in your sins (disbelief). Here John stresses the eternal importance of knowing who Jesus really is and believing that.

The sixth occurrence of the I, I AM witness continues

in this same narrative with the Jews in John 8:25-29

They clearly did not know what He was saying or who He was. "Who are you?"

Jesus responded, "Just what I have been saying to you from the beginning. I have many things to say and to judge concerning you, but He who sent Me is true; and I speak to the world those things which I heard from Him."

They still did not understand that He spoke to them about the Father.

Then Jesus said to them, "When you lift up the Son of Man, then you will know that *I, I AM,* and I do nothing of Myself; but as My Father taught Me, I speak these things. And He who sent Me is with Me. The Father has not left Me alone, for I always do those things that please Him."

Many believed in Him as He spoke these things.

The seventh occurrence of the I, I AM theme is in John 8:48-59

We need to look at this occurrence in a larger context in chapter 8. The Jew accused Jesus of being a Samaritan and having a demon. Jesus defended Himself saying, "I do not have a demon; but I honor My Father, and you dishonor Me. And I do not seek My glory; there is One who seeks and judges. Most assuredly, I say to you, if anyone keeps My word he shall never see death."

The Jews vehemently reacted to this notion. "Now we know that You have a demon! Abraham is dead, and the prophets; and You say, 'If anyone keeps My word he shall never taste death.' Are You greater than our father Abraham, who is dead? And the prophets are dead."

Imagine if you can the animated gestures of the Jews when they sarcastically asked, "Who do You make Yourself out to be?"

Jesus contended that He is not honoring Himself, but it is His Father who honors Him. "Your father Abraham rejoiced to see My day, and he saw it and was glad."

What do you mean Abraham saw it? "You are not yet fifty years old, and have You seen Abraham?"

It appears Jesus guided this conversation in such a way to make this bold claim. "Most assuredly, I say to you, before Abraham was, *I, I AM.*"

At this point they picked up stones to throw at Him. Why did this infuriate them so? We skip ahead to John 10:33 for the answer. "For a good work we do not stone You, but for blasphemy, and because You, being a Man, make Yourself God."

There we have it! The Jews themselves believed Jesus was claiming to be God by declaring, *I, I AM* He.

> *The eighth occurrence of the I, I AM witness is in John 10:1-6*

Jesus identified Himself as the door of the sheep. Whoever came before Him were thieves and robbers. Then, He said, "*I, I AM* the door. If anyone enters by Me, he will be saved, and will go in and out and find pasture."

The ninth occurrence of the I, I AM witness immediately follows in John 10:11-16

Jesus not only is the door of the sheep, He is the good shepherd of the sheep. "*I, I AM* the good shepherd. The good shepherd gives His life for the sheep." He further noted, "I am the good shepherd; and I know My sheep, and am known by My own. As the Father knows Me, even so I know the Father; and I lay down My life for the sheep. And other sheep I have which are not of this fold; them also I must bring, and they will hear My voice; and there will be one flock and one shepherd."

The tenth occurrence of the I, I AM witness is in John 11:25-26

Jesus uses the death and resurrection of his friend, Lazarus, to announce, "*I, I AM* the resurrection and the life. He who believes in Me, though he may die, he shall live. And whoever lives and believes in Me shall never die."

Amazing! Then He surveyed His onlookers and asked this piercing question, "Do you believe this?"

The eleventh occurrence of the I, I AM witness is in John 14:1-5

Jesus exhorted his followers not to be troubled with His imminent death and departure. "You believe in God, believe also in Me. In My Father's house are many mansions; if it were not so, I would have told you. I go to prepare a place for you, and if I go and prepare a place for you, I will come again and receive you to Myself; that where *I, I AM*, you may be also. And where I go you know, and the way you know."

Thomas said to Him, "Lord, we do not know where You are going, and how can we know the way?"

"*I, I AM* the way, the truth, and the life. No one comes to the Father except through Me."

Breaking this down line-by-line, might give us a different perspective on what Jesus was saying.

1. Jesus came from the Father and is returning to the Father.
2. In Father's house are many mansions.
3. Jesus goes to prepare a place for us *in Father's house.*
4. Jesus will come again and receive us unto Himself *in Father's house.*
5. Where He is we will be also *in the Father.*

The twelfth occurrence of the I, I AM witness is in John 15:1-8

Jesus illustrated it this way. "*I, I AM* the true vine, and

My Father is the vinedresser. Every branch in Me that does not bear fruit He takes away; and every branch that bears fruit He prunes, that it may bear more fruit. You are already clean because of the word which I have spoken to you."

The thirteenth occurrence of the I, I AM witness is in John 18:1-6

Jesus was in the garden at the time of his betrayal. Judas led a detachment of troops and officers from the chief priests and Pharisees to Jesus. Jesus knowing all things that would come on Him, asked them, "Whom are you seeking?"

"Jesus of Nazareth," they answered.

"I, I AM."

The scripture narrative tell us that when Jesus said *I, I AM*, "they drew back and fell to the ground."

Jesus asked them a second time, "Whom are you seeking?"

And again they answered, "Jesus of Nazareth."

Again, Jesus answered, "I have told you that *I, I AM*."

Have you ever asked why they drew back and fell to the ground when Jesus announced that He was *I, I AM*? Perhaps they became aware they were in the presence of Yahweh and fell to the ground. Or, perhaps, being in the presence of the Great *I, I AM*, they fell to the ground.

This should leave little doubt to the jury in this court room that Jesus was who he said He Himself claimed to be.

This Jesus is the One in whom John invites us to believe and this is what we are to believe about Him. "In the beginning was the Word [Jesus], and the Word was with God, and the Word was God."

The "*I, I AM*" witness steps down from the witness stand, but remains under oath and can be recalled anytime.

Witness Three

Witnesses of Jesus

John calls to the stand various *Witnesses* to testify of Jesus.

John, the apostle, is not content with merely declaring that Jesus is the Logos [Word], the *I, I AM*, the Son of God. He sets out like a skilled lawyer, giving a defense in the courtroom of unbelief. He provides further proof by calling various witnesses to the stand; namely, John the Baptist, Jesus' works, the scriptures, Moses, God the Father, a blind man, Pilate, and himself.

Numerous signs, wonders, and miracles punctuated the verbal debate between Jesus and His accusers. These miracles alone, however, did not prove sufficient evidence for these Jews. Jesus constantly gave the Jews excuses to challenge Him. He used various occasions to proclaim who He was, why He came, and what people must do with Him.

The religious Jews followed Him around, incessantly arguing against His authenticity. These Jews played an essential role in the courtroom drama of Jesus' defense. Against these accusations, Jesus built the defense of His own claim. Without them, His case would have been more challenging to prove.

Our attention is drawn to this debate between the Jews and Jesus. Various witnesses are next to take the stand.

His first witness is John the baptizer   John 1:6-34

John, the apostle, said of John, the baptizer, that he had been sent from God to bear witness of Jesus, the Light through whom all might believe. John the baptizer was not that light, but was sent to bear witness of that Light.

John the baptizer had gone out to the people who were coming to him in repentance to be baptized. On one such occasion Jesus showed up. John saw Him coming toward him, and announced, "Behold! The Lamb of God who takes away the sin of the world! This is He of whom I said, 'After me comes a Man who is preferred before me, for He was before me. I did not know Him; but that He should be revealed to Israel, therefore I came baptizing in water.'"

John continued his witness, saying, "I saw the Spirit descending from heaven like a dove, and He remained upon Him. I did not know Him, but He who sent me to baptize with water said to me, 'Upon whom you see the Spirit descending, and remaining on Him, this is He who baptizes with the Holy Spirit.' And I have seen and testified that this is the Son of God."

Jesus continued to point to John, the baptizer, as a witness in John 5:31-35. Jesus contended that if He bore witness of Himself, His witness would not have been true, but there was another one who bore witness of Him whose witness was true. "You have sent to John, and he has borne witness to the truth."

Nevertheless, Jesus insisted He did not receive testimony from man. "John was the burning and shining lamp, and you were willing for a time to rejoice in his light."

His second witness is the very works that Jesus did
John 5:36-38

Jesus presented a greater witness than that of John. They were the works the Father had given Him to finish—"the very works that I do bear witness of Me, that the Father has sent Me."

"The Father Himself, who sent Me, has testified of Me. You have neither heard His voice at any time, nor seen His form. But you do not have His word abiding in you, because whom He sent, Him you do not believe."

His third witness is the Scriptures   John 5:39-40

The Scripture in Jesus time was the Jewish Bible, called the Tanach, commonly referred to by Christians as the Old Testament.

Jesus said to the Jews, "You search the Scriptures, for in them you think you have eternal life; and these are they which testify of Me. But you are not willing to come to Me that you may have life."

The forth witness is Moses   John 5:45-47

Jesus had no need to personally accuse the Jews, because they were already accused by Moses. They claimed to have trusted in Moses, yet Moses spoke of Jesus. Consequently, Jesus said, "If you believed Moses, you would believe Me; for he wrote about Me. But if you do not believe his writings, how will you believe My words?"

The fifth witness is the Father   John 8:13-20

Earlier, Jesus said that if He bore witness of Himself, His witness would not be true.

The Pharisees, nonetheless, accused Him of that very thing. "You bear witness of Yourself; Your witness is not true."

"Even if I bear witness of Myself, My witness is true, for I know where I came from and where I am going; but you do not know where I come from and where I am going. You judge according to the flesh; I judge no one. And yet if I do judge, My judgment is true; for I am not alone, but I am with the Father who sent Me.

"It is also written in your law that the testimony of two men is true. I am One who bears witness of Myself, and the Father who sent Me bears witness of Me."

"Where is Your Father?"

"You know neither Me nor My Father. If you had known Me, you would have known My Father also."

Jesus spoke these things in the temple treasury. No one laid hands on Him because His hour had not yet come.

Again, in John 8:54-55 Jesus acknowledged if He honored Himself, His honor would be nothing. Rather, He said, "It is My Father who honors Me, of whom you say that He is your God. Yet you have not known Him, but I know Him. And if I say, 'I do not know Him,' I shall be a liar like you; but I do know Him and keep His word."

The sixth witness is a blind man given sight   John 9

John goes into much detail relating the testimony of a man who, having been born blind, received His sight. Jesus acknowledged to His disciples that this man's blindness was not due to his nor his parents sins, but that the works of God should be revealed in Him. Jesus was bound to do the works of God who sent Him.

The blind man who was made well had to convince his neighbors that he was the same man they used to know. He explained, "A Man called Jesus made clay and anointed my eyes and said to me, 'Go to the pool of Siloam and wash.' So I went and washed, and I received sight."

They brought the man to the Pharisees and an argument

pursued between them and the man. The man explained to them again that it was Jesus who did this thing.

The Pharisees denounced Jesus saying, "This Man is not from God, because He does not keep the Sabbath."

However, others argued, "How can a man who is a sinner do such signs?"

The Pharisees said to the blind man again, "What do you say about Him because He opened your eyes?"

"He is a prophet."

Still, the Jews did not believe concerning him, so they questioned his parents. They confirmed their son had been born blind, but out of fear of the Jews, they sent the Jews back to him. They interrogated him further, then eventually put him out of the synagogue. He would not say what they wanted to hear.

Jesus heard they had cast him out of the synagogue. When Jesus found him, He said to him, "Do you believe in the Son of God?"

"Who is He, Lord, that I may believe in Him?"

"You have both seen Him and it is He who is talking with you."

He broke before the Lord. "Lord, I believe!" And he worshiped Him.

Jesus used this incident to say, "For judgment I have come into this world, that those who do not see may see, and that those who see may be made blind." Given the context of this statement, this saying likely refers to those who think they are accepted because they consider themselves descendants of Abraham. The credential for acceptance is not based on genealogy, but on faith.

The seventh witness is Pilate John 18:1-19:22

John calls Pilate to take the stand. The question at hand here has to do with Jesus being the King of the Jews. (The setting of this witness has been established in the beginning of this study titled, *The Setting*.)

Jesus is arrested in Gethsemane, taken before the High priest, and questioned. He is led to the Praetorium and goes up before Pilate. Pilate goes back and forth between Jesus and the Jews, appearing to argue the case in favor of Jesus. The Jews want to put Him to death, but Pilate finds no fault in Him.

"Are You the King of the Jews?"

Jesus retorted, "Are you speaking for yourself about this, or did others tell you this concerning Me?"

Yes. He is the King of the Jews, but Jesus explains that His Kingdom is not of this world. "If My kingdom were of this world, My servants would fight, so that I should not be delivered to the Jews; but now My kingdom is not from here."

"Are You a king then?"

"You say rightly that I am a king. For this cause I was

born, and for this cause I have come into the world, that I should bear witness to the truth. Everyone who is of the truth hears My voice."

Pilate declared to the Jews again saying, "I find no fault in Him at all." And they demanded the release of Barabbas.

Pilate scourged Jesus. The soldiers twisted a crown of thorns and put it on His head and draped a purple robe across His shoulders. They jeered, "Hail, King of the Jews!"

Then, they crucified Jesus.

Pilate wrote a title and had it put on the cross.

JESUS OF NAZARETH,

THE KING OF THE JEWS

It was written in Hebrew, Greek, and Latin.

The chief priests of the Jews took exception to it and tried to persuade Pilate not to write, "The King of the Jews," but, He said, "I am the King of the Jews."

At this point, Pilate gives his final judgment. "What I have written, I have written." And so it went down in history!

Pilate, as a high profile witness, in an authentic court of law, delivered his final judgment upon Jesus saying, "I find no fault in Him," declaring also that He was the King of the Jews.

The eighth witness is John, the apostle himself   John 21:20-25

By writing this narrative, John put himself on the stand as a firsthand witness of all that he heard and saw.

John was the disciple Jesus loved, who had leaned on Jesus' breast at the last supper. He was the one of whom Peter inquired of the Lord, "What about this man?"

Jesus answered, "If I will that he remain till I come, what is that to you? You follow Me."

John, referring to himself wrote, "This is the disciple who testifies of these things, and wrote these things; and we know that his testimony is true. And there are also many other things that Jesus did, which if they were written one by one, I suppose that even the world itself could not contain the books that would be written."

The *Witnesses of Jesus* step down from the witness stand, but remains under oath and can be recalled anytime.

Witness Four
Believe

John calls the *Believe* witness to the stand.

Jesus declared, even before His death on the cross, that He not only finished the works of God, but that He was the finished work of God. He testified that He was God—the *I, I AM* who existed before Abraham. Furthermore, in John's courtroom, numerous witnesses took the stand in defense of His claim.

Now, the question is: What is to be done with this Jesus? What is the proper response to Him, if indeed He is the *I, I AM*—the finished work of God?

John contends that if Jesus has finished works of God, what is there left for us to do? His contention is that the only work we can do is to believe in Him. John's conclusion is encapsulated in John 6:28-29. Those who witnessed Jesus healing the man born blind asked, "What shall we do, that we may work the works of God?"

Jesus affirmed, "This is the work of God, that you believe in Him whom He sent."

All God wants from us is to believe in Him through His

Son Jesus. Failure to believe in Jesus is the same as calling Him a liar. God hates to be called a liar. We shall see in later themes, however, that if we truly believe in Jesus, He will change our paradigms, our lives, and our behaviors. Nevertheless, we begin with this pivotal theme of believing. People who truly believe in Him, follow Him.

The entire book of John is devoted to bringing his reader to one decision. "…that you may believe that Jesus is the Christ, the Son of God, and that believing you may have life in His name." John 20:31. Certain events, therefore, will be highlighted as this witness is questioned.

John, the baptizer   John 1:6-9

John, the apostle, introduces this "believing" theme at the beginning of his gospel narrative. He said of John, the baptizer, "This man came for a witness, to bear witness of the Light, that all through him might believe."

Believing is a verb. Faith is a noun. Believing is the action of faith. Believing, according to John's understanding, is equivalent to receiving. If we truly believe Jesus, we will receive Him.

John, the baptizer preached, "He came to His own, and His own did not receive Him. But as many as received Him, to them He gave the right to become children of God, to those who believe in His name."

Nathanael   John 1:43-51

Jesus went to Galilee and found a man called Philip. Jesus said to him, "Follow Me."

"Philip was from Bethsaida, the city of Andrew and Peter. Philip found Nathanael and said to him, 'We have found Him of whom Moses in the law, and also the prophets, wrote—Jesus of Nazareth, the son of Joseph.'

"Can anything good come out of Nazareth?" Nathanael puzzled.

"Come and see."

Jesus saw Nathanael coming toward Him and affirmed, "Behold, an Israelite indeed, in whom is no deceit!"

"How do You know me?" Nathanael asked.

"Before Philip called you, when you were under the fig tree, I saw you."

"Rabbi, You are the Son of God! You are the King of Israel!'

"Because I said to you, I saw you under the fig tree, do you believe? You will see greater things than these. Most assuredly, I say to you, hereafter you shall see heaven open, and the angels of God ascending and descending upon the Son of Man."

Nathanael believed, received, and followed. His paradigm was changed. His life was changed.

Nicodemus John 3:1-21

John makes his case on the importance of believing in the dialogue between Jesus and a man named Nicodemus who was a Pharisee and a ruler of the Jews. Here, we learn much about faith.

Nicodemus came to Jesus under the cover of dark to inquire of Him. A private face-to-face took place about the need to be born again. This "born again" theme will be presented later. This idea of being born again feeds into the issue of faith.

Nicodemus is puzzled. "How can these things be?"

The carnal mind objects. We want things explained. We argue. Do not pass it off by telling me to just "believe." Yet, that was precisely Jesus' response. Count the times the term "believe" occurs in the following narrative by Jesus to Nicodemus.

"We speak what We know and testify what We have seen, and you do not receive." Receiving is believing.

"If I have told you earthly things and you do not *believe*, how will you *believe* if I tell you heavenly things?

"As Moses lifted up the serpent in the wilderness, even so must the Son of Man be lifted up, that whoever *believes* in Him should not perish but have eternal life. For God so loved the world that He gave His only begotten Son, that whoever *believes* in Him should not perish but have everlasting life. For God did not send His Son into the world to condemn the world, but that the world through Him might be saved.

"He who *believes* in Him is not condemned; but he who does not *believe* is condemned already, because he has not *believed* in the name of the only begotten Son of God."

Again, we see it all hinges on believing. Nevertheless, we also see that when one truly believes, he receives Jesus and eternal life. His life is changed. He has been given a different kind of life.

John nails down this point. "He who *believes* in the Son has everlasting life; and he who does not *believe* the Son shall not see life, but the wrath of God abides on him." John 3:36.

Faith brings about a good result and unbelief brings about a bad result. Passivity is not an option. Failure to believe is a decision not to believe with serious consequences.

Samaritans   John 4:1-42

Jesus came to a city of Samaria and encountered a Samaritan woman at Jacob's well. He asked her for a drink. His disciples had gone into the city for food. She questioned Him, "How is it that You, being a Jew, ask a drink from me, a Samaritan woman?" The Jews had no dealings with the Samaritans.

Jesus proceeded to tell her that whoever drinks of the water that He gives will never thirst again and it "will become in him a fountain of water springing up into everlasting life."

The woman asked for this water and Jesus set her up. "Go, call your husband, and come here."

She answered, "I have no husband."

Jesus said to her, "You have well said, 'I have no husband,' for you have had five husbands, and the one whom you now have is not your husband; in that you spoke truly."

After further discussion, the woman left her water pot, went back into the city, and said to the men, "Come, see a Man who told me all things that I ever did. Could this be the Christ?"

The Samaritans went out to Him and many of them of that city believed in Him "because of the word of the woman who testified, 'He told me all that I ever did.'"

The Samaritans urged Jesus to stay with them. He stayed two days and many more believed because of His word.

The message John wants us to get is simply this. They believed. "Then they said to the woman, 'Now we believe, not because of what you said, for we ourselves have heard Him and we know that this is indeed the Christ, the Savior of the world.'"

A Nobleman's Son   John 4:46-53

Jesus came again to Cana of Galilee where He had turned the water into wine. "A certain nobleman from

Capernaum was there whose son was sick. When he heard that Jesus had come out of Judea into Galilee, he went to Him and implored Him to come down and heal his son who was at the point of death.

Jesus said to him, "Unless you people see signs and wonders, you will by no means believe."

The nobleman responded, "Sir, come down before my child dies!"

Jesus said, "'Go your way; your son lives.' So the man believed the word that Jesus spoke to him, and he went his way. And as he was now going down, his servants met him and told him, saying, 'Your son lives!'"

The Nobleman asked them the hour when he got better. They said to him, "Yesterday at the seventh hour the fever left him."

"The father knew it was at the same hour in which Jesus said to him, 'Your son lives.'" The nobleman and his whole household believed.

John did not say that this event changed their lives, but why else would he have told this story? All that was said of them is that they believed.

Peter's confession   John 6:41-71

The Jews complained about Jesus saying that He was the bread of life. He shocked them even more so when He said, "unless you eat the flesh of the Son of Man and drink His blood, you have no life in you." This was such a hard saying that many of His followers went back and did not follow Him anymore.

Jesus said to the twelve, "Do you also want to go away?"

"Simon Peter answered Him, 'Lord, to whom shall we go? You have the words of eternal life. Also we have come to believe and know that You are the Christ, the Son of the living God.'"

It seems like a simple matter to believe, but it is not. Such faith is costly. To believe in Jesus Christ, the *I, I AM,* costs us our lives.

Blind man given sight   John 9:7

On several occasions, Jesus mixed believing with some kind of action. The action was a demonstration of faith. Jesus required the blind man to whom He gave sight to wash in the pool of Siloam. The man did as Jesus said and came back with his sight.

Later on in this story, Jesus heard that the Jews had put him out of the synagogue. He found him and asked, "Do you believe in the Son of God?"

The man asked, "Who is He, Lord, that I may believe in Him?"

Jesus said to him, "You have both seen Him and it is He who is talking with you."

"Lord, I believe!" He declared and worshiped Him.

Lazarus   John 11:1-26

John takes us to Bethany, the town of Mary, Martha, and their brother, Lazarus. Lazarus had died and they sent for Jesus. He delayed going there because He intended to make a statement that He was the resurrection and the Life. He would prove this by raising Lazarus from the dead.

Jesus went there after Lazarus had been in the tomb four days.

Many of the Jews were with Martha and Mary to comfort them.

When Martha heard that Jesus was coming, she went out to meet Him. She said to Him, "Lord, if You had been here, my brother would not have died. But even now I know that whatever You ask of God, God will give You."

"Jesus said to her, 'Your brother will rise again.'

"I know that he will rise again in the resurrection at the last day."

Jesus seized the moment to declare, "*I, I AM* the resurrection and the life. He who believes in Me, though he may die, he shall live. And whoever lives and believes in Me shall never die. Do you believe this?"

The more important question is, "Do we believe that Jesus is the Resurrection and the Life?"

Many rulers believed   John 12:42-50

Belief in Jesus has to be without compromise. John

reported that many of the rulers believed in Jesus, but did not confess Him because they did not want to be put out of the synagogue. John noted, "They loved the praise of men more than the praise of God."

This stirred Jesus to cry out, "He who believes in Me, believes not in Me but in Him who sent Me. And he who sees Me sees Him who sent Me. I have come as a light into the world, that whoever believes in Me should not abide in darkness. And if anyone hears My words and does not believe, I do not judge him; for I did not come to judge the world but to save the world. He who rejects Me, and does not receive My words, has that which judges him—the word that I have spoken will judge him in the last day."

If we believe in Jesus, we receive Him. If we do not believe in Him, we reject Him; thus, bringing judgment down upon ourselves.

Jesus, praying to the Father said, "For I have given to them the words which You have given Me; and they have received them, and have known surely that I came forth from You; and they have believed that You sent Me." John 17:8.

It is as simple and difficult as that. Believe. Receive. Follow.

The "Believe" witness steps down from the witness stand, but remains under oath and can be recalled anytime.

Witness Five
The Son of God

John calls *The Son of God* witness to the stand.

This witness defies common sense. How is it logical that Jesus could be Yahweh *(I, I AM)* and at the same time be the Son of Yahweh? This was not a problem for John. He never bothered to reconcile this difference. (Unless, John explained this in the "In Him" witness taking the stand later on.)

Once again, we return to the beginning of John's gospel to follow this witness as it interlaces with many of the other witnesses throughout. We learn a few things about the Son of God as we leaf through the references below.

Only the Son has seen the Father   John 1:14, 18

John continued his prologue regarding the divinity of Jesus declaring, "The Word became flesh and dwelt among us, and we beheld His glory, the glory as of the only begotten of the Father, full of grace and truth...."

John, the baptizer, confirmed that Jesus was the one of whom he said, "He who comes after me is preferred before me, for He was before me." John said this in full knowledge that he was born before Jesus. What could he mean, "He was before Me?"

John added, "Of His fullness we have all received." John, the apostle continued to testify, "And grace for grace. For the law was given through Moses, but grace and truth came through Jesus Christ."

Then, Jesus is distinguished from all others. "No one has seen God at any time. The only begotten Son, who is in the bosom of the Father, He has declared Him."

The Son of God is the Lamb of God   John 1:29

As John was baptizing in the Jordan for the repentance of sin one day, Jesus approached him. John proclaimed that Jesus was the Lamb of God who takes away the sin of the world.

The word "sin" in the Greek has also been translated "sinful" and "offense." It means, among other things, to be without a share in something, to miss the mark, to err, be mistaken, to wander from the path of uprightness. Jesus took this sin away.

The Son of God baptizes in the Holy Spirit   John 1:31-34

The baptizer witnessed the Holy Spirit descending from heaven like a dove and remaining on Jesus. He clarified that while he baptized in water, Jesus is He who would baptize in the Holy Spirit.

The baptizer further witnessed, "I have seen and testified that this is the Son of God."

The Son of God is the King of Israel   John 1:49-51

We return to Nathanael who recognized Jesus saying, "Rabbi, You are the Son of God! You are the King of Israel!"

Jesus responded to him and said, "Because I said to you, 'I saw you under the fig tree,' do you believe? You will see greater things than these." Jesus prophesied, "Most assuredly, I say to you, hereafter you shall see heaven open, and the angels of God ascending and descending upon the Son of Man."

The "Son of Man" terminology is used synonymously with "Son of God" designation.

The Son of God is the only begotten Son   John 3:18

Jesus is distinguished from other "sons" of God by the identification of being "the only begotten Son of God." God is He who brought Jesus into the world.

Jesus explained to Nicodemus, "He who believes in Him is not condemned; but he who does not believe is condemned already, because he has not believed in the name of the only begotten Son of God."

Believe in the Son   John 3:36

Belief is in the Son of God. "He who believes in the Son has everlasting life; and he who does not believe the Son shall not see life, but the wrath of God abides on him."

The dead will hear the voice of the Son   John 5:25

Jesus, "Most assuredly, I say to you, the hour is coming, and now is, when the dead will hear the voice of the Son of God; and those who hear will live."

Father has His seal on the Son   John 6:27

Jesus, "Do not labor for the food which perishes, but for the food which endures to everlasting life, which the Son of Man will give you, because God the Father has set His seal on Him."

Jesus is the Son of the living God   John 6:69

Peter, "Also we have come to believe and know that You [Jesus] are the Christ, the Son of the living God." The Son of God is the Messiah.

Jesus declared Himself to be the Son of God   John 9:35-38

Jesus heard that they had cast the blind man out; and when He had found him, He said to him, "Do you believe in the Son of God?"

He answered saying, "Who is He, Lord, that I may believe in Him?"

Jesus answered, "You have both seen Him and it is He who is talking with you."

Then he said, "Lord, I believe!" And he worshiped Him.

The Son of God is God   John 10:36-39

The Jews accused Jesus because He considered Himself to be God by calling Himself "The Son of God." In their renewed efforts to stone Jesus, He challenged them saying, "Many good works I have shown you from My Father. For which of those works do you stone Me?"

The Jews answered, "For a good work we do not stone You, but for blasphemy, and because You, being a Man, make Yourself God."

Jesus asked, "Is it not written in your law, 'I said, You are gods'? If He called them gods, to whom the word of God came (and the Scripture cannot be broken), do you say of Him whom the Father sanctified and sent into the world, 'You are blaspheming,' because I said, 'I am the Son of God'? If I do not do the works of My Father, do not believe Me; but if I do, though you do not believe Me, believe the works, that you may know and believe that the Father is in Me, and I in Him."

Therefore they sought again to seize Him, but He escaped their hand.

This connection between the Son of God being God occurs in John 19:5-7. Pilate presented Jesus to the Jews wearing a crown of thorns and the purple robe. "Behold the Man!"

The chief priests and officers shouted, "Crucify Him! Crucify Him!"

Pilate tried to reason. "You take Him and crucify Him,

for I find no fault in Him."

The Jews answered him, "We have a law, and according to our law He ought to die, because He made Himself the Son of God."

Even when John states his purpose for writing the gospel, he makes that connection between the Son of God and the Messiah. "These are written that you may believe that Jesus is the Christ, the Son of God, and that believing you may have life in His name." John 20:31.

The glory of the Son and God's glory   John 11:4

The glory the Son of God brings upon the Father reflects back upon the Son as well. When Jesus heard that Lazarus had died, He said, "This sickness is not unto death, but for the glory of God, that the Son of God may be glorified through it."

John 13:31 concurs. Judas had left the supper to betray Jesus, at which time Jesus informed the others that now was the time the Son of Man was to be glorified. He was referring to His death on the cross. He noted also that God would be glorified in Him. "If God is glorified in Him, God will also glorify Him in Himself, and glorify Him immediately."

The Son of God is Messiah   John 11:17-27

Jesus arrived at Bethany where Martha, Mary, and others had come to comfort them concerning Lazarus' death. A conversation took place between Martha and Jesus.

"Lord, if You had been here, my brother would not have died. But even now I know that whatever You ask of God, God will give You."

Jesus pronounced, "Your brother will rise again."

Martha responded, "I know that he will rise again in the resurrection at the last day."

Jesus revealed, "I am the resurrection and the life. He who believes in Me, though he may die, he shall live. And whoever lives and believes in Me shall never die."

Then, He asked her directly, "Do you believe this?"

This is where we see a definitive statement linking the Son of God with the Messiah. "Yes, Lord," she answered. "I believe that You are the Christ [Messiah], the Son of God, who is to come into the world."

The "Son of God" witness steps down from the witness stand, but remains under oath and can be recalled anytime.

Witness Six

Descend and Ascend

John calls the *Descend and Ascend* witness to the stand.

The previous witnesses testified that Jesus not only finished the works of God, but also is the work of God inasmuch as He is the Great *I, A*M. Others testified that He is the Messiah in whom we are to believe. Then, we heard the witness declaring Him to be the Son of God.

The question before the court now has to do with His origin. From where did He come? He claimed to have descended from above. (Heaven is above. The world is below.)

As might be expected, this claim played into the hands of the blasphemy charge against Him.

Jesus testified that He knew where He came from and where He was going. This witness aims to settle that question.

The Holy Spirit descends upon Jesus   John 1:19-34

Initially, John presents evidence that the Holy Spirit descended from heaven to validate Jesus as the Messiah.

The Jews and Levites had been sent to find out from John, the baptizer, what he had to say about himself. John clearly denied that he was the Messiah, Elijah, or the Prophet, but that he was the "voice of one crying in the wilderness, make straight the way of the Lord."

Jesus appeared where John was baptizing and John declared, the "Lamb of God who takes away the sin of the world." He explained that this Jesus was preferred before him because He came before him. What could this mean since John was actually born before Jesus?

John further explained, "I did not know Him, but He who sent me to baptize with water said to me, 'Upon whom you see the Spirit descending, and remaining on Him, this is He who baptizes with the Holy Spirit.' And I have seen and testified that this is the Son of God."

Jesus, being the Son of God, came before John.

Angels ascending, descending upon Son of Man
John 1:51

Not only did the Holy Spirit descend from heaven, but also the angels are revealed to have descended and ascended upon the Son of Man.

Jesus called Philip to follow Him to Galilee, the city of Andrew and Peter. Later, Andrew and Peter found Nathanael and said to him, "We have found Him of whom Moses in the law, and also the prophets, wrote—Jesus of Nazareth, the son of Joseph."

Jesus saw Nathanael coming toward Him and amazed him with a word of knowledge, leading to Nathanael's confession. "Rabbi, You are the Son of God! You are the King of Israel!"

Jesus prophesied to him saying, "Most assuredly, I say to you, hereafter you shall see heaven open, and the angels of God ascending and descending upon the Son of Man."

Nathanael was a notable person in the eyes of Jesus and Jesus was pleased to let him know it. More so, Jesus knew the angels were validating Him as the Messiah in this way—ascending and descending upon Him. For this to be known to others strengthened the testimony that He was the Messiah. Nathanael was a reliable witness.

The Son of man is from heaven   John 3:13

Now, we see the claim that the Son of man descended from heaven.

We revisit Nicodemus and his conversation with Jesus. The main point in this dialog had to do with the need to be born again. This concept was puzzling to Nicodemus. "How can a man be born when he is old? Can he enter a second time into his mother's womb and be born?"

That which is born of the flesh is flesh, Jesus explained, but that which is born of the Spirit is spirit.

Nicodemus was still puzzled, "How can these things be?"

Jesus answered him, "Are you the teacher of Israel, and do not know these things? Most assuredly, I say to you, We speak what We know and testify what We have seen, and you do not receive Our witness. If I have told you earthly things and you do not believe, how will you believe if I tell you heavenly things? No one has ascended to heaven but He who came down from heaven, that is, the Son of Man who is in heaven."

In this statement, Jesus announced that He came down from heaven, declaring He was the Son of Man (God). The Son of Man is He who descended from and ascends to heaven.

He who comes from above is above all   John 3:31

The Jews and the disciples of John, the baptizer, were arguing over the question of purification because the disciples of Jesus were baptizing more than John and all the people were going to Him.[3]

John reasserted he was not the Messiah, but that he had been sent beforehand to declare the Messiah. One evidence that Jesus was the Messiah is embedded in His origin and destiny. John declared, "He who comes from above is above all; he who is of the earth is earthly and speaks of the earth. He who comes from heaven is above all."

The bread from heaven   John 6:33-51

The searching crowd found Jesus in Capernaum and wanted to know when He got there. In typical Jesus

---

[3] Immersing (bathing) people in water is a Jewish tradition for purification. It is called mikveh. In a broader sense mikveh means a collection of water.

fashion, He answered the deeper question at hand. "You seek Me, not because you saw the signs, but because you ate of the loaves and were filled." He charged them not to seek food that perishes, but that "which endures to everlasting life, which the Son of Man will give you."

"Most assuredly," Jesus said, "Moses did not give you the bread from heaven, but My Father gives you the true bread from heaven. For the bread of God is He who comes down from heaven and gives life to the world...For I have come down from heaven, not to do My own will, but the will of Him who sent Me."

"Lord, give us this bread always," they said.

Still, the Jews complained because He said He was the bread that came down from heaven. "Is not this Jesus, the son of Joseph, whose father and mother we know? How is it then that He says, 'I have come down from heaven'?"

Jesus said it again. He not only was the bread of life, He was the *living* bread that came down from heaven. The word *living* is from the Greek *zoe*, having to do with the God-kind of life.

  See the Son of man ascend   John 6:62.

That Jesus was the bread from heaven was a hard saying even for His disciples. "Who can understand?"

"Does this offend you?" Jesus asked. "What then if you should see the Son of Man ascend where He was before?"

Jesus not only descended from heaven, but knew He would ascend back to heaven to the Father and His disciples would witness it.

They knew where Jesus was from   John 7:27-19.

It seemed essential for the disciples of Jesus to believe He descended from above and would again ascend, and it appeared they came to believe it.

However, the issue of Jesus' origin was still in question with the Jews. They knew where Jesus was from regarding His natural birth, but admitted, "When the Christ comes, no one knows where He is from."

The disconnect between what the Jews knew to be Jesus' earthly origin and that of the Messiah's fed into their disbelief. Even though Jesus natural birth was in Bethlehem, He was, nonetheless, sent from above. Jesus knew where He was from and was answering their question. He essentially was saying, "When the Christ comes, *you will know* where He is from—above, heaven, sent by the Father."

Jesus, while teaching in the Temple shouted out, "You both know Me, and you know where I am from; and I have not come of Myself, but He who sent Me is true, whom you do not know. But I know Him, for I am from Him, and He sent Me."

Jesus defends His self-witness   John 8:14

The Pharisees accused Jesus of bearing witness of

Himself; thereby, nullifying His claim.

As far as Jesus was concerned they could accept His witness or not. "Even if I bear witness of Myself, My witness is true, for I know where I came from and where I am going; but you do not know where I come from and where I am going."

Jesus cited their own law that says the testimony of two men is true. Jesus bore witness of Himself and the Father who sent Him bore witness of Him.

They had to ask, "Where is Your Father?"

"You know neither Me nor My Father. If you had known Me, you would have known My Father also."

Jesus predicts His departure   John 8:23

Jesus told them again He was going away and they would seek Him, but would die in their sin (disbelief). "Where I go you cannot come."

The Jews thought He meant to kill Himself because He said they could not go where He was going.

Jesus declared it again. "You are from beneath; I am from above. You are of this world; I am not of this world. Therefore I said to you that you will die in your sins; for if you do not believe that I am He, you will die in your sins."

Jesus knew His destiny   John 13:3

Jesus and His disciples were together for His last supper

with them. It was before the Feast of Passover. Jesus knew His hour had come and that He would depart the world to return to the Father, "having loved His own who were in the world, He loved them to the end."

The devil had already put it into Judas's heart to betray Jesus.

Jesus knew the Father had given all things into His hands. He knew He had come from God and was going to God.

Others could not immediately go with Him   John 13:36

Jesus descended from the Father and told His disciples He would ascend again to the Father.

Peter asked, "Lord, where are You going?"

Jesus told them they could not go with Him at that time, but they would follow Him afterward.

Characteristic of Peter, he wanted to know why he could not go with Him. He vowed, "I will lay down my life for Your sake." On that occasion, Jesus foretold of Peter's denial of Him.

The only way to Father is through the Son   John 14:1-28

Jesus made clear to His followers that the only way they could ascend to the Father with Him would be through Him. He was going to prepare a place for them. If He went, He would come again and receive them to Himself. "That where I am, you may be also.

And where I go you know, and the way you know."

As He ascended to the Father, so would they also because Jesus is the way, the truth, and the life. No one comes to the Father except through Him. Jesus was their ascension.

"You have heard Me say to you, 'I am going away and coming back to you.' If you loved Me, you would rejoice because I said, 'I am going to the Father,' for My Father is greater than I."

The disciples believed   John 17:8-25

Jesus was talking to the Father and acclaimed He had given His followers the words the Father had given Him. He knew He had come forth from the Father. His followers also had come to believe Jesus had been sent from the Father.

Jesus prayed for those whom the Father had given Him. All who belonged to Jesus belonged to the Father. All who belonged to the Father belonged to Jesus. Jesus was glorified in them. He extended this prayer to all those who would believe in Him through their word.

Then He prayed, "Father, I desire that they also whom You gave Me may be with Me where I am, that they may behold My glory which You have given Me; for You loved Me before the foundation of the world. O righteous Father! The world has not known You, but I have known You; and these have known that You sent Me."

The disciples believed and have the promise to be where Jesus is, ascended to the Father.

Jesus ascended to His Father   John 20:17

After Jesus was crucified and resurrected, but prior to His ascension into heaven, Mary went to the garden to inquire about Jesus. Jesus appeared to her and said, "Do not cling to Me, for I have not yet ascended to My Father; but go to My brethren and say to them, 'I am ascending to My Father and your Father, and to My God and your God.'"

So far as John and this witness is concerned, this question of origin is settled. Jesus descended from the Father and ascended again to the Father, thus, authenticating that He is the Messiah, the Son of God.

The *Descend and Ascend* witness steps down from the witness stand, but remains under oath and can be recalled anytime.

Witness Seven
Eternal Life

John calls the *Eternal Life* witness to the stand.

The decision to believe in and follow Jesus has the gift of eternal life as its end result. Time again Jesus claimed that he who believed in Him would have eternal life. Believe and have!

John began his gospel witness by declaring, "In the beginning was the Word, and the Word was with God, and the Word was God." John is referring to Jesus as the Word. "He was in the beginning with God. All things were made through Him, and without Him nothing was made that was made." Then, John declares, "In Him was life, and the life was the light of men."

This word for "life" in the Greek is *zoe* and translates "life." Other words for life in the Greek are *bios*, having to do with biological life and *psuche*, having to do with soul life. *Zoe* has to do with spirit life. Simply stated, *zoe* is the God-kind of life and can only be received as a gift from God through Jesus who is this life. *Zoe* life, being the essence of God, has no beginning or ending.

Therefore, John speaks of this *zoe* life as eternal or

everlasting. Eternal is from the Greek *aionius*. It has been translated, eternal, everlasting, since the world began, and forever. Eternity life has no beginning or end. It is that which has always been and always will be. The Greek words for eternal life combined are *aionius zoe*.

Nicodemus   John 3:1-36

High on the list of everyone's favorite verses of scripture is John 3:16, one that we as believers take for granted. Yet, it is one that is not fully appreciated. "For God so loved the world that He gave His only begotten Son, that whoever believes in Him should not perish but have everlasting life."

The simply theology set forth here is believe in Jesus, the only begotten Son, and have everlasting life. Believe and have! Even though God did not send His Son into the world to condemn the world, the fact remains that one who does not believe in the Son whom God sent, condemns himself. He does not have eternal life. "He who believes in the Son has everlasting life; and he who does not believe the Son shall not see life, but the wrath of God abides on him."

This eternal life occurs when we, through faith, are born again. Jesus told Nicodemus that he must be born again. John had already established this in the beginning of his gospel saying, "He came to His own, and His own did not receive Him. But as many as received Him, to them He gave the right to become children of God, to those who believe in His name: who were born, not of blood, nor of the will of the flesh, nor of the will of man, but of God." John 1:11-13.

The Samaritan Woman   John 4:1-14

We return to Jacob's well in Samaria where Jesus engages the Samaritan woman who came to draw water. His disciples had gone into the city to buy food.

Jesus made a distinction between the water from the well and the water that He would give to those who believe in Him.

"Whoever drinks of this water will thirst again, but whoever drinks of the water that I shall give him will never thirst. But the water that I shall give him will become in him a fountain of water springing up into everlasting life."

Believing in Jesus is the same as receiving Him. Receiving Him is to receive His life—the God-kind of life—springing up from within.

The Bread of Life   John 6:22-69

In the beginning of his gospel, John identified Jesus as the Word of God and that this word was the life, and the life was the light.

Here, in this narrative, Jesus reveals Himself as the bread of life, the bread from Heaven. Jesus not only gives us eternal life, but He gives it by giving of Himself.

Jesus said to those who were following Him, "Moses

did not give you the bread from heaven, but My Father gives you the true bread from heaven. For the bread of God is He who comes down from heaven and gives life to the world."

Then they said to Him, "Lord, give us this bread always."

Jesus does not just give *zoe*, He is the bread of life, the bread of *zoe*." He continued to say, "I am the living bread which came down from heaven. If anyone eats of this bread, he will live forever; and the bread that I shall give is My flesh, which I shall give for the life of the world." The words *living* and *live* are from the root word *zoe*.

Jesus made it known that this is the will of Him who sent Him, "that everyone who sees the Son and believes in Him may have everlasting life; and I will raise him up at the last day."

Jesus continued to hammer the point with the Jews who objected to Him saying He was the bread which came down from heaven.

The concept of Jesus being the bread of *zoe* plunges us into deeper waters. Believing has always carried with it the idea of receiving. Now, Jesus talks about eating His flesh. "the bread that I shall give is My flesh, which I shall give for the life of the world."

The Jews quarreled among themselves saying, "How can this Man give us His flesh to eat?"

Moreover, Jesus said, if you do not eat His flesh and drink His blood you do not have His life in you, but whoever eats His flesh and drinks His blood has eternal life and Jesus will raise Him up at the last day.

"As the living Father sent Me, and I live because of the Father, so he who feeds on Me will live because of Me. This is the bread which came down from heaven—not as your fathers ate the manna, and are dead. He who eats this bread will live forever."

After this, many of His disciples turned from following Him. Jesus asked His twelve, "Do you also want to go away?"

Simon Peter answered Him, "Lord, to whom shall we go? You have the words of eternal life. Also we have come to believe and know that You are the Christ, the Son of the living God."

We see, then, according to John, that following Jesus involves more that having a passive belief system about Him. It is a matter of consuming Him and being consumed by Him.

Resurrection and the Life   John 11:1-44

Jesus not only is eternal life, He is also the Resurrection. He used the occasion of Lazarus' death to make this declaration. He backed up His claim by raising Lazarus from the dead.

Jesus was on His way to Bethany where Lazarus, Mary, and Martha lived. When He heard that Lazarus was sick, Jesus said, "This sickness is not unto death, but for the glory of God, that the Son of God may be glorified through it."

Jesus had not yet gone into the city and Lazarus had already been in the tomb four days. Martha said to Jesus, "Lord, if You had been here, my brother would not have died. But even now I know that whatever You ask of God, God will give You."

Jesus said to her, "Your brother will rise again."

Martha said to Him, "I know that he will rise again in the resurrection at the last day."

At this point, Jesus revealed to her saying, "I am the resurrection and the life (*zoe*). He who believes in Me, though he may die, he shall live (*zoe*). And whoever lives (*zoe*) and believes in Me shall never die."

Mary came to where Jesus was and fell down at His feet, saying to Him, "Lord, if You had been here, my brother would not have died."

Later, Jesus came to the tomb and instructed them to remove the stone. Martha warned, "Lord, by this time there is a stench, for he has been dead four days."

Jesus said to her, "Did I not say to you that if you would believe you would see the glory of God?"

They removed the stone and Jesus lifted up His eyes and said, "Father, I thank You that You have heard Me. And I know that You always hear Me, but because of the people who are standing by I said this, that they may believe that You sent Me."

Now when He had said these things, He cried with a loud voice, "Lazarus, come forth!" And he who had died came out bound hand and foot with grave clothes, and his face was wrapped with a cloth. Jesus said to them, "Loose him, and let him go."

In so doing, Jesus showed He not only could raise people from the dead, but He also is the resurrection and the life (*zoe*).

The Way, Truth, and Life   *John 14:1-19*

John is easing us into a deeper revelation of Jesus as the Life. Jesus told His disciples not to be troubled. Note the sequence: "In My Father's house are many mansions. I go to prepare a place for you. I will come again and receive you to Myself." The mansions are in the Father. Where Jesus is we will be also, in the Father. He "is the way, the truth, and the life (*zoe*)."

Eternal life defined   *John 17:1-3*

Jesus is the life. He went to prepare a place for them/us. That place is in Him in the Father.

He prayed, "Father, the hour has come. Glorify Your Son, that Your Son also may glorify You, as You have given Him authority over all flesh, that He should give eternal life to as many as You have given Him.

At this point, the progression is complete. Jesus clearly defined what is eternal life. "This is eternal life, that they may know You, the only true God, and Jesus Christ whom You have sent." If we have eternal life in Christ we will know the Father. If we know the Father, it is because we have eternal life. There is no other way to know God.

We believe and are born again. We receive His eternal life. That eternal life is knowing the Father who sent the Son in whom we are to believe.

Eternal life is not just something for the future after we die. It is a present reality in the life of every true believer. It is given at the time we believe and receive. "Whoever eats My flesh and drinks My blood has eternal life, and I will raise him up at the last day." John 6:54. This is why Jesus could say, "Whoever lives [*zoe*] and believes in Me shall never die."

The "Eternal Life" witness steps down from the witness stand, but remains under oath and can be recalled anytime.

Witness Eight

In Him

John calls the *In Him* witness to the stand.

In questioning this witness, John plainly records Jesus' claim that He is eternal life. When Jesus gives us eternal life as the result of our faith in Him and in His name, He gives us of Himself. In this, we come to abide in Him—He in us and we in Him. Jesus was most passionate about us knowing this. This revelation is life altering. We, the jury, must see this!

Logos   John 1:1-2

John began this defense in His opening statement.

The point John argues here regarding Jesus is profound and absolute. Our oneness with Jesus begins with Jesus' oneness with the Father. The following points establish His oneness:

1. In the beginning was the Word (logos).
2. The Word was with God.
3. The Word was God.
4. He was in the beginning with God.

Logos, according to Britannica.com, is the Greek for "word," "reason," or "plan." In Greek philosophy and theology, it is the term that refers to the divine reason implicit in the cosmos that orders it and gives it form and meaning. John deliberately asserted that what the Greeks understood to be the logos was in reality, Jesus. Jesus is the divine reason in the cosmos who ordered it and gave it form and meaning.

Moreover, Jesus knew "that the Father had given all things into His hands and that He had come from God and was going to God." John 13:3.

John skillfully builds his case, progressing from the beginning of his gospel toward the end. At this point, he makes to case that receiving eternal life is the same as receiving Jesus.

Into Him   John 3:16

The *In Him* reality is embedded in this beloved passage. "For God so loved the world that He gave His only begotten Son, that whoever believes in Him should not perish but have everlasting life."

We have always taken this translation for granted. We who grew up in church have quoted it from childhood. "Whosoever believes *in* Him...." Believing *in* Jesus, however, can be rather cerebral and passive, even religious. To merely say "in Jesus" fails to do justice to the original Greek. The preposition "in" is usually translated from the Greek *en*. However, the preposition John uses in this verse is *eis*, not *en*. *Eis* has been more frequently translated "into." That is a huge difference. Believing in Jesus is far more than a matter of simply believing *about* Him or believing *in* Him. It is a matter of believing *into* Him. When we believe *into* Him, we become one with Him.

Bread of Life   *John 6:48-56*

The *In Him* understanding takes on more traction in the discourse where Jesus declares He is the bread of life. He explained to them that their fathers ate the manna in the wilderness, yet they are dead. He, on the other hand, is the bread that came down from heaven and whoever eats of it will not die. Now, if He is the bread that came down from heaven—the bread of which they can eat—then they would be partaking of Him. He is the living bread. The bread that He offered was His flesh. Can you imagine how offensive this would have been to kosher Jews?

Naturally, the Jews quarreled among themselves. "How can this Man give us His flesh to eat?"

Then Jesus said to them, "Most assuredly, I say to you, unless you eat the flesh of the Son of Man and drink His blood, you have no life in you. Whoever eats My flesh and drinks My blood has eternal life, and I will raise him up at the last day. For My flesh is food indeed, and My blood is drink indeed."

He continued to declare the believer's oneness with Him. "He who eats My flesh and drinks My blood abides in Me, and I in him."

Thirst   John 7:37-39

Prior to the passage about His flesh and His blood, John told the story of Jesus and the Samaritan woman at Jacob's well quoting Jesus, "Whoever drinks of the water that I shall give him will never thirst. But the water that I shall give him will become in [Greek *en*] him a fountain of water springing up into [Greek *eis*] everlasting life." John 4:14.

Later in Jerusalem, on the last day of a great feast day, Jesus cried out, saying, "If anyone thirsts, let him come to Me and drink. He who believes *into* (Greek, *eis*) Me, as the Scripture has said, out of his heart will flow rivers of living water." But this He spoke concerning the Spirit, whom those believing into Him would receive; for the Holy Spirit had not yet been given, because Jesus had not yet been glorified.

Way, Truth, and Life   John 14:6-11

Jesus said to Thomas who questioned where Jesus was going. "Lord, we do not know where You are going, and how can we know the way?"

Jesus was going to the Father and the only way to the Father was through Jesus who is the way, the truth, and the life.

Jesus further explained, "If you had known Me, you would have known My Father also; and from now on you know Him and have seen Him."

Philip said to Him, "Lord, show us the Father, and it is

sufficient for us."

Jesus said to him, "Have I been with you so long, and yet you have not known Me, Philip? He who has seen Me has seen the Father; so how can you say, 'Show us the Father'? Do you not believe that I am in (*en*) the Father, and the Father in (*en*) Me? The words that I speak to you I do not speak on My own authority; but the Father who dwells in (*en*) Me does the works. Believe Me that I am in (*en*) the Father and the Father in (*en*) Me, or else believe Me for the sake of the works themselves."

Father is greater John 14:28

John had no problem quoting Jesus saying the Father and the Son were one and at the same time saying the Father is greater than the Son. "You have heard Me say to you, 'I am going away and coming *back* to you.' If you loved Me, you would rejoice because I said, 'I am going to the Father,' for My Father is greater than I."

It should be no mystery to us either. We are in Christ and Christ is in us, making us one with Him as He and the Father are one; yet, we also know that Christ is greater by far than we.

Vine John 15:1-8

John advances this *In Him* defense further. Jesus wants us to know how our relationship in Him works and how we are able to bear fruit.

The following points establish our oneness with Jesus.
1. Jesus is the true vine.
2. The Father is the vinedresser.
3. We are the branches.
4. Every branch that does not bear fruit Father takes away.
5. Every branch that bears fruit still has to be pruned by Father.
6. We are clean because of the word He has spoken to us.
7. We are to abide in Him and He in us.
8. Because, the branch cannot bear fruit by itself.
9. He is the vine and we are the branches. When we abide in Him and He in us, we bear much fruit.
10. Anyone who does not abide in Him is cast out as a branch and withers, gathered up and thrown into the fire.
11. Moreover, if we abide in Him and His words abide in us, we will ask what we desire and it shall be done for us. It is doubtful we will be asking for self-interest things.
12. By this, the Father is glorified and we will be His disciples.

All who believe into Jesus belong to the Father and all who belong to the Father belong to Jesus. John 17:10.

Though Jesus left us in the world, He prayed, "Holy Father, keep through Your name those whom You have given Me, that they may be one as We are." John 17:11.

Jesus prayed this *oneness* prayer for all believers at all times. Moreover, it stands to reason if we are one in Him as He is one in us individually, we are one with each other. We just are! It is not something we have to make happen. It is something we need to recognize and act on accordingly. John 17:20-21.

If, indeed, we are in Him, He is in us, and we with one another, we will be with Him and will participate in His glory. John 17:22. We will be made perfect in one. All this so the world may know the Father had sent Jesus and has loved us as He has loved Jesus. John 17:23.

Do you believe we are one with Jesus and the Father because we are in Him and He is in us? Do you believe that Jesus' prayer is being answered? If so, then we believe the Father is keeping us.

The "In Him" witness steps down from the witness stand, but remains under oath and can be recalled anytime.

Witness Nine

The Holy Spirit

John calls the *Holy Spirit* witness to the stand.

The purpose of calling the Holy Spirit to the stand is to answer, "How?" How can this God-kind of life given to us through God's Son, Jesus, abide in us?

Jesus' baptism by John, the baptizer   John 1:29-34

The activity of the Holy Spirit is first mentioned in John's gospel at the time John, the baptizer, was baptizing in the Jordan. John saw Jesus coming toward him and proclaimed, "Behold! The Lamb of God who takes away the sin of the world! This is He of whom I said, 'After me comes a Man who is preferred before me, for He was before me.' I did not know Him; but that He should be revealed to Israel, therefore I came baptizing with[4] water."

Then John "saw the Spirit descending from heaven like a dove, and He remained upon Him." John further explained while he baptized in water, Jesus is the one

---

[4] The preposition "with" in this translation is the Greek word *en* most frequently translated "in." It has also been translated "by," "with," "among," "at," "on," and "through." Translating *en* in this context, given the imagery of baptism (immersion), in this context, the Greek *en* would be more accurately translated "in." John baptized in water.

who baptizes *in* the Holy Spirit. John puts himself on record saying, "I have seen and testified that this is the Son of God." John did not know Jesus, but as He confessed, "He who sent me to baptize with water said to me, 'Upon whom you see the Spirit descending, and remaining on Him, this is He who baptizes with the Holy Spirit.'"

Samaritan woman: God is spirit   John 4:23-24

Jesus and His disciples traveled to Samaria. His disciples had gone into town to buy food. Jesus was left alone at Jacob's well when a Samaritan woman approached. He used this opportunity to inform her (as well as us today) that "the hour is coming, and now is, when the true worshipers will worship the Father in spirit and truth; for the Father is seeking such to worship Him."

Jesus explained that "God is Spirit, and those who worship Him must worship in spirit and truth." The Spirit of God is the Holy Spirit. They are the same. If God is spirit, then the Holy Spirit is God. John had no issue believing this.

We see here that any true worship of God has to be in the Spirit and by the Spirit of God. This is the kind of worship God seeks.

The Spirit gives life   John 6:63

Jesus told his audience "It is the Spirit who gives life; the flesh profits nothing. The words that I speak to you are spirit, and they are life."

Out of the heart   John 7:37-39

Jesus made reference to the activity of the Holy Spirit on the last day, that great day of the feast, when He stood and cried out, saying, "If anyone thirsts, let him come to Me and drink. He who believes in Me, as the Scripture has said, out of his heart will flow rivers of living water."

He spoke this concerning the Spirit, whom those believing in Him would receive; for the Holy Spirit was not yet given, because Jesus was not yet glorified.

The Holy Spirit as Helper   John 14:15-18; 26

As John's witness progresses he quoted Jesus giving more information regarding the necessary role of the Holy Spirit in our lives. "If you love Me," Jesus said, "Keep My commandments. And I will pray the Father, and He will give you another Helper[5], that He may abide with you forever—the Spirit of truth, whom the world cannot receive, because it neither sees Him nor knows Him; but you know Him, for He dwells with you and will be in you."

The Work of the Holy Spirit   John 16:5-15

Jesus, while still reclining with His disciples at the last

---

[5] The word helper in the Greek is *parakletos* (Paraclete) and has also been translated Comforter. It refers to one who is called to one's side, to one's aid; one who pleads another's cause before a judge like a counsel for the defense.

meal, told of the things that were about to happen to Him—that He would soon go away to God who sent Him. None asked Him where He was going because sorrow had filled their hearts. He assured them it was to their advantage that He should go away because He would send the Helper to them—the Holy Spirit. Jesus noted several advantages for sending the Holy Spirit. These are:

"And when He has come, He will convict the world of sin, and of righteousness, and of judgment: of sin, because they do not believe in Me; of righteousness, because I go to My Father and you see Me no more; of judgment, because the ruler of this world is judged."

Many other things could be said to them, but they could not bear them at the time. The role of the Holy Spirit would guide them into all truth saying. "He will not speak on His own authority, but whatever He hears He will speak; and He will tell you things to come. He will glorify Me, for He will take of what is Mine and declare it to you."

Finally, regarding the role of the Holy Spirit, He said, "All things that the Father has are Mine. Therefore I said that He [the Holy Spirit] will take of Mine and declare it to you."

Jesus breathed on them to receive the Holy Spirit
John 20:22

This is the last John says about the role of the Holy

Spirit. John knew the Holy Spirit would be the means by which the life and love of Christ would abide in His believers and they in Him, and be one with Him even as He and the Father are one.

Everything we are authorized to do in the name of Jesus is accomplished by the work of the Holy Spirit. Everything! The Father sent the Son to finish the Father's work. Once Jesus accomplished that, He returned to the Father and sent the Holy Spirit.

The Holy Spirit does it all. We are born again by the Spirit. We are baptized in the Holy Spirit. We worship in Spirit and truth. The Spirit gives life. The Spirit flows out of our hearts as living water. He teaches all things and brings all things to our remembrance. He is our comforter and helper. He abides with us forever, dwelling with us and in us. He is the Spirit of truth. He testifies of Jesus. He convicts the world of sin, righteousness, and judgment. He will take all things of Jesus and declare it to us. He sanctifies (separates) us by His truth.

The "Holy Spirit" witness steps down from the witness stand, but remains under oath and can be recalled anytime.

Witness Ten

Love

J ohn calls the *Love* witness to the stand.

This love witness also stands as John's closing argument to the jury.

Trial arguments normally progress toward a conclusion in which the counselors attempt to prove the guilt or innocence of the person on trial. What a counselor concludes, therefore, becomes the paramount argument he or she intends to make.

John's defense of the claims Jesus made of Himself is no different. In the case of John's gospel, all things about Jesus culminate in love. He introduced the love witness in John 3:16 and ended it in John 21.

Based on the emphasis and summation of his defense, John believes the most significant aspect of God's nature is His love and is the main message of the life and death of Jesus.

Moreover, if we abide in Jesus and Jesus abides in us, just as He and the Father abide in each other, then the love that we express is sourced out of the very life of God.

What about this God kind of love? The Greek language

has several words that are translated "love" in the English. John uses two of these. The verb forms are: *phileo* and *agapeo*. *Phileo* means "friendship" and includes loyalty to friends, family, and community. It is the Greek word for affection and is strongly associated with emotions. *Phileo* brings pleasure to the one expressing the love, usually expecting something in return.

John 12:25 is an interesting look at the use of *phileo*. Jesus said, "He who loves (*phileo*) his life (*psuche*) will lose it, and he who hates his life (*psuche*) in this world will keep it for eternal life."

The Greek word *psuche* applies to our soul life. The word *phileo* relates to *psuche*. It is the kind of love or affection we would identify with soul life. *Phileo* is soulish in nature. In order for us to keep our souls for eternal life, we have to hate it. The word hate means hate.

Agape, on the other hand, is spirit life. It is the God-kind of love demonstrated by the very life and death of our Savior, Jesus Christ. Jesus defined *agape*-love by saying, "Greater love has no one than this, than to lay down one's life for his friends." John 15:13.

Based on how it has been lived out in scripture, my personal definition of *agape* is as follows: *Agape* is the unconditional, sacrificial giving of oneself for what is in the best interest of another without expecting anything in return."[6]

John unfolds his witness of love by showing how intertwined it is in relationships.

God loves the world: Nicodemus   John 3:10-18

John initially calls love to the stand in the story of Nicodemus, the Pharisee.

Three of John's witnesses are expressed in this story of Nicodemus: love, faith, and eternal life. They are all connected. However, the initial point John makes regarding the love theme simply begins with, "God so loved the world..."

Jesus expressed to Nicodemus the need to be born again, a concept that Nicodemus found hard to grasp. Nicodemus was thinking worldly. "How can a man be born when he is old? Can he enter a second time into his mother's womb and be born?" Most Christians today think of being born again as being given a second chance to start over. Jesus had something far better in mind. He was talking about being born by a life that has its source in God.

"For God so loved the world that He gave His only begotten Son, that whoever believes into Him should not perish but have everlasting life. For God did not send His Son into the world to condemn the world, but that the world through Him might be saved. He who

---

[6] A more thorough look into *agape* is found in my book, *Stepping in the Circle*.

believes into Him is not condemned; but he who does not believe is condemned already, because he has not believed in the name of the only begotten Son of God."

Points from this narrative are:

1. Love is the very nature of God.
2. Jesus came from God as a demonstration of His love.
3. The simple response of the world is to believe into Jesus.
4. The reward of believing into Jesus is eternal life.
5. The consequences of rejecting this love is condemnation.
6. Men condemn themselves because they love (*agapeo*) the darkness more than the light, because their deeds are evil. Given our definition of *agape*, this would read, "because men unconditionally and sacrificially gave themselves to the world...."

People who know God have the love of God in them. Jesus knows when the love of God is in us and when it is not. The love of God is that which we possess and that by which we are possessed. John 5:42.

Father loves the Son   John 5:20

Jesus already declared how the Father loves the Son to the extent that He has given all things into His hand. John 3:35.

God not only loved the world that He sent His only begotten Son, but we read here in John 5:20 that He also loved the Son.

"For the Father loves the Son, and shows Him all things that He Himself does; and He will show Him greater works than these, that you may marvel." The Greek word for "loves" in this verse is *phileo*. The Father not only *agapeo* the Son, but also *phileo* Him. He has both that sacrificial and affectionate love for the Son.

Moreover, Father loves the Son because He laid down His life that He might take it up again. John 19:17. How can we humanly understand this concept that God loved His Son so much that He sent Him to die for our sins? We understand this when we realize God was not sacrificing His Son. He was the sacrifice Himself. That is the nature of the God-kind of love.

The Son loved His disciples   John 13:1

Prior to the Feast of the Passover and the washing of His disciple's feet, John reports that Jesus knew His hour had come and would depart from this world to the Father. John made known that Jesus loved His own who were in the world and loved them to the end.

His disciples love one another   John 13:2-35

While gathered for this meal, Jesus washed His disciple's feet. Judas was still present. Jesus was troubled in His spirit and told them that one among them would betray Him. This is the scene in which it is told that the one whom Jesus loved was leaning on His bosom. John was speaking of himself. Leaning back on Jesus' breast, John asked Jesus, "Lord, who is it?"

After Judas had gone out, Jesus told the rest of them that He, the Son of man is glorified and God is glorified in Him. He told them He would be going to a place they could not go. Because He was going, He gave them a new commandment, "that you love one another; as I have loved you, that you also love one another. By this all will know that you are My disciples, if you have love for one another."

He who loves the Son keeps His commandments   John 14:15; 21-24

Jesus associated obedience with *agape*. He said, "If you love Me, keep My commandments. This love is a circle of relationships all around. The points here are:

1. He who has Jesus' commandments and keeps them is he who loves Him.
2. He who loves Jesus will be loved by His Father.
3. Jesus will love the one who loves Him and will manifest (reveal) Himself to him.
4. He who loves Jesus will keep His word.
5. He who loves Jesus and keeps His word is He to whom Jesus and the Father will come. Jesus and the Father will make their home with him.

The Son loves the Father   John 14:31

Jesus concludes this part of His narrative saying, "But that the world may know that I love the Father, and as the Father gave Me commandment, so I do. Arise, let us go from here."

His disciples abide in His love   John 15:1-17

Abiding in the vine is abiding in Jesus. Abiding in Jesus is the only way we can produce the fruit of love.

Jesus said, "I am the true vine, and My Father is the vinedresser. Every branch in Me that does not bear fruit He takes away; and every branch that bears fruit He prunes, that it may bear more fruit.... As the Father loved Me, I also have loved you; abide in My love. If you keep My commandments, you will abide in My love, just as I have kept My Father's commandments and abide in His love. These things I have spoken to you, that My joy may remain in you, and that your joy may be full. This is My commandment, that you love one another as I have loved you."

Then, Jesus claimed as His friends those who did whatever He commanded them. "No longer do I call you servants, for a servant does not know what his master is doing; but I have called you friends, for all things that I heard from My Father I have made known to you.... You did not choose Me, but I chose you and appointed you that you should go and bear fruit, and that your fruit should remain, that whatever you ask the Father in My name He may give you."

Jesus made clear His command—"that you love one another."

Hated by the world   John 15:19

However, if He loves us and we love Him and one another, we will be hated by the world.   "If you were of the world, the world would love (*phileo*) its own. Yet because you are not of the world, but I chose you out of the world, therefore the world hates you."

Father affectionately loves those who affectionately love the Son   John 16:27

"For the Father Himself loves you, because you have loved Me, and have believed that I came forth from God." *Phileo* is used both times in this verse. *Agape* is that unconditional, sacrificial giving of one's self and appears to be short on feelings. Nevertheless, we are assured here that our relationship with the Father and the Son also involves affection. Those warm and tender feelings for God and Jesus are good and have their place in our relationship with the Father and the Son.

Agape is the life of God in us   John 17:23

This God-kind of love can only exist when Jesus is in us. When He is in us, then His love is made perfect and the world will know that the Father sent the Son, and the Father loves us as He loved the Son. Jesus continued in His prayer, "I have declared to them Your name, and will declare it, that the love with which You loved Me may be in them, and I in them."

Agape will be tested   John 21:15-18

Peter had sworn never to abandon Jesus. Jesus knew better. He prophesied to Peter that he would deny Him three times. And so he did! Peter thought he was capable of *agape*—making that unconditional, sacrificial commitment to the Lord. Jesus knew it had to be tested.

Later, after His resurrection, Jesus was with His followers. John tells the story. The nuance of this story is lost in the English translation.

After they had eaten breakfast, Jesus asked Simon Peter, "Simon, son of Jonah, do you love Me more than these?" The word for love here is *agape*.

"Yes, Lord; You know that I love You." The word for love here is *phileo*. After his denial of Jesus in the court yard, how could Peter ever confess *agape*, but he could not deny *phileo*.

Nevertheless, Jesus said to him, "Feed My lambs."

Jesus asked Peter a second time, "Simon, son of Jonah, do you love (*agapeo*) Me?"

Peter answered the same, "Yes, Lord; You know that I love (*phileo*) You."

Again, Jesus charged him saying, "Tend My sheep."

Then, Jesus asked him a third time. This time, however, Jesus responded with *phileo*. Who can say what might have been the tone of His voice in asking this question? "Simon, *son* of Jonah, do you love (*phileo*) Me?"

Peter was grieved because He said to him the third time, "Do you love (*phileo*) Me?"

And he said to Him, "Lord, You know all things; You know that I love (*phileo*) You."

Jesus said to him the third time, "Feed My sheep."

Years later, Peter, by the power of *apape*-love within him was able to make that sacrifice of his life.

Jesus predicted Peter's death. "Most assuredly, I say to you, when you were younger, you girded yourself and walked where you wished; but when you are old, you will stretch out your hands, and another will gird you and carry you where you do not wish." Tradition has it that Peter felt himself unworthy to be put to death in the same manner as Jesus and requested to be crucified upside down.

John summarizes his case with this *agape*-love effect.

Agape love, the God-kind of love, is the ultimate witness of the authenticity of this Jesus who claimed to be the Son of God. His love is the proof.

The progressive points of this love-witness are:

1. God first loved the world.
2. He loved the Son.
3. The Son loved His disciples.
4. The disciples love one another and keep His commandments.
5. The Father loves those who love the Son.
6. The Son loves the Father.
7. His followers abide in His love (in Him).
8. The world will hate His followers.
9. This love is in us and we are being made perfect in one.
10. Finally, this love will be tested and found faithful.

The love we are to have for God in Christ and for each other has to be God's love. We can only possess His love by abiding in Him and He in us.

The "Love" witness steps down from the witness stand, but remains under oath for eternity.

The Summation And Sequestration

John was well aware this trial could not have had any other outcome. All that happened to Jesus happened because, "It is written." Therefore, let us not judge the religious Jews or the crowd in Jesus' time that sent Him to the cross. All of it was necessary. Ultimately, we have to conclude that Divine Providence sent Jesus to the cross. Nonetheless, that does not leave us guiltless.

Here is the twist in this case!

Jesus was accused of blasphemy for saying He was the Son of God. The prosecutors in this case did not believe it to be true. In their minds, He deserved to be crucified. The purpose of the prosecution therefore was to prove Him guilty of blasphemy.

The purpose of the defense was to disprove the blasphemy charge against Jesus on the conviction that He was who He said He was—the Son of God, even God.

The Prosecution's [Plaintiff's] closing argument

I stand here before you in the crux of your personal life to prove beyond a shadow of doubt that this Jesus on trial here today is guilty of blasphemy because He said He was the Son of God, even God.

It is true Pilate found no fault in Jesus; however, please note that He is not on trial for breaking a Roman law such that would justify punishment by death. Rather, He is on trial for breaking the law of Moses according to the Jews. You heard them say, "We have a law, and according to our law He ought to die, because He made Himself the Son of God." John 19:7. Consequently, Pilate released Him to the Jews, allowing them to take Him and crucify Him because he himself found no fault in Him.

Therefore, I ask you to consider this man's own words and deeds in light of Moses' law according to the Jews, which leave no doubt that the Jews had a lawful right to seek His death. I present a few of the many offenses as proof of His guilt.

He healed a man on the Sabbath. John 5:16; John 7:23. "Blasphemy!" "We have a law!"

He also said that God was His father, making Himself equal to God. John 5:18. "Blasphemy!" "We have a law!"

He said He was the bread that came down from heaven. John 6:41-42. "Blasphemy!" "We have a law!"

He said the bread that He gave was His flesh, which He claimed was for the life of the world. John 6:51-52. John 7:1. "Blasphemy!" "We have a law!"

He said He knew the Father because He claimed to be from Him and even more so that God had sent Him. John 7:28-29. "Blasphemy!" "We have a law!"

He accused the Jews of not being the children of Abraham because they did not do the works of Abraham. John 8:37-41. "Blasphemy!" "We have a law!"

He said He was the *I, I AM*, existing even before Abraham, He deserved to be stoned. John 8:58-59. "Blasphemy!" "We have a law!"

He said that He was the good shepherd. John 10:19. "Blasphemy!" "We have a law!"

He, being a man, made Himself God. John 10:31-33. "Blasphemy!" "We have a law!"

All of these things and more! He, being a mere man, claimed to be the finished works of God. He claimed to be the *I, I AM*. He claimed to be the Son of God. He claimed to have come from God and was returning to God. He claimed to be the way, the truth, and the life. He claimed to be the resurrection from the dead. He claimed to be in the Father as the Father was in Him, and that those who believe would likewise be in Him and He in them.

Even in view of the numerous signs, wonders, and miracles He allegedly performed, how could any man make such claims?

Therefore, I submit to you the only verdict you can

return is guilty. Guilty of blasphemy.

The defense's closing argument

Ladies and Gentlemen of the jury. There sits before you a man from Galilee who came among you preaching and teaching the Kingdom of God with attesting signs and wonders. The Prosecution is correct in reporting what Jesus said of Himself. We do not deny those accusations, but would add a few other things He said and did as well.

Jesus declared to you that He not only came to do the Father's works, but He was the finished works of God. He declared that he was the Great *I, I AM* who was known as Yahweh to our forefathers. He presented various others beyond Himself as witnesses of His divinity. He spoke of the need to believe that He was the Son of God. He demonstrated how He was the Resurrection and the Life. He taught how believing into Him resulted in our being in Him and He in us, even as He and the Father are one. He attested to the promise and power of the Holy Spirit whom He would send. He not only spoke of the love of God, but He was the ultimate demonstration of God's love, and how we are to love as He loved. He sealed all of these claims with signs, wonders, and miracles. Then, He arose from the dead to put the final punctuation mark on His claim."

"And there are also many other things that Jesus did, which if they were written one by one, I suppose that even the world itself could not contain the books that would be written." John 21:25.

Therefore, we disagree with the prosecution's claim that this man committed blasphemy by saying He is the Son of God, even God. The defense argues that this man is the Son of God, even God.

You as the jury in this case must return a verdict of not guilty of blasphemy. In so doing, you will be declaring with multitudes of other believers that, indeed, this Jesus is the Christ [Messiah] the Son of the Living God, even God.

The Prosecutors and the Defense rest their cases

The Judge instructs the jury

The charge against this man is clear. The issue at hand is not whether the defendant is the Son of God, but did He commit blasphemy by saying He was the Son of God. If you return a verdict of guilty, you will be agreeing with the prosecution that He committed blasphemy and is worthy of the death penalty. In effect, you will be saying you do not believe He is the Son of God.

If, on the other hand, you return a verdict of not guilty, you will be determining that He did not commit blasphemy. In that event you will be acknowledging that this man truly is the Son of God. You will identify yourself as a believer and follower of Him.

The Jury Room

The Jury retires to the jury room with the preceding instructions. Each juror, sequestered in the jury room of his or her own heart, will decide to believe or not to believe that this man, Jesus, is who He said He was.

Is the evidence presented by the prosecution sufficient to convict this man of blasphemy? Did John, the defense attorney for Jesus, make a convincing case?

The verdict of the jury will determine the sentence by the Judge. In this trial, each of us, individually, are both jury and judge. John's testimony will be believed by some and condemned by others.

The irony, however, is this. If indeed He is the Son of God, even God, in condemning Him by our disbelief, we stand condemned, not Him. The sentence is not about His life, but ours. The trial was as much about us as it was about Him. The sentence we pronounce upon Him, will determine the sentence we pronounce upon ourselves. We commit ourselves either to eternal life or condemnation.

These are the things to which John gave testimony with the single purpose: "that you may believe that Jesus is the Christ, the Son of God, and that believing you may have life in His name." John 20:31.

What is your verdict?

Books by Charles Elliott Newbold, Jr.

The Crucified Ones: Calling Forth the End-Time Remnant intends to call forth a people to walk in radical obedience in preparation for the Lord's coming.

His Presence in the Midst of You: Calling Forth a Sanctified People, written in first person from God's perspective, is a book that intends to call forth a sanctified people to carry the ark of the Lord's Presence.

The Harlot Church System: Come Out of Her My People exposes how we have made idols of self-worship out of these Things we call "church" and echoes God's call to His remnant to "come out of her My people."

In Search of Dad: Calling Forth the Dad Within the Man is a book that intends to call forth that supernatural, transcending power that flows from Father-God, enabling men to be godly fathers to their families.

The Transcendent Seed of Abraham: A People for Yahveh illustrates the difference between the covenant made with Abraham and the covenant made with Moses, and how Jesus/Yeshua made good on God/Yahveh's promise to Himself to form a people for Himself. (74 page booklet)

Stepping into the Circle of all that pertains to the Kingdom of God is a book that expresses the need for us to begin living our lives out from within the Kingdom of God.

Streams That Make Glad is a series of pastoral articles first published in Validity Magazine, Hohenwald, Tennessee USA.

Sayings is a collection of thoughts that Charles has had for over thirty-five years while sitting before the Lord and listening to His still small voice.

These books may be purchased in paperback at Amazon.com or in electronic form on iBooks, Kindl e, and Nook. Additional information may be seen on www.charlesnewbold.com.

Made in the USA
Las Vegas, NV
30 June 2021